Currency Risk
Management

Currency Risk Management

Alfred Kenyon
The Plessey Company

JOHN WILEY & SONS

Chichester · New York · Brisbane · Toronto

British Library Cataloguing in Publication Data:

Kenyon, Alfred
  Currency risk management.
  1. Foreign exchange administration
  2. Risk management
  I. Title
  332.4'5   HG3853.R/

  ISBN 0 471 10003 X

Phototypeset by Input Typesetting Ltd., London
and printed at Pitman Press, Bath

Contents

Foreword

We often hear the reflection that a child "had not asked to be born." Well, this book certainly asked to be written. I tried to suppress it, but it kept taunting me that if I did not write it, I could never sort out my ideas about the topic. So I had to give in.

That is not to say that the birth was easy. Many colleagues and fellow treasurers nobly assisted me. Derek Hawkins, now with Inmos, particularly helped enormously by wading through the first version and preserving me from all manner of errors. I must also single out John Heywood of Hambros Bank, who nobly read through the whole manuscript and gave invaluable advice, and Jocelyn Monk of the same bank who so efficiently read the proofs.

And of course, but for the unbelievable patience and tolerance of my long-suffering wife and family, the book could certainly not have seen the light of day.

It is dedicated to them.

CHAPTER 1

Introduction

Why another book about the management of currency risk? The literature is not without distinguished contributions from practising treasurers, although it could probably do with some more. Nor does this book enjoy a more favoured vantage point than other books written by such treasurers, except perhaps that it can draw on rather more experience of large export tenders and contracts than some other books.

No, if this book has something new to add to an understanding of currency risk and its management, it lies in its endeavour to reach a more systematic and cohesive view of the topic. It would be much too pretentious to call this an attempt at a theory of currency risk. We are looking at an art rather than a science. Its structure is riddled with pragmatic considerations. But this book is an attempt to explain how the house is built, the parts that go to make the whole, the method of construction, and how all these fit into its architectural design. In describing the way the house has been constructed, we may not enumerate every tapwasher or light fitting, but we should gain an insight into the purpose of all the parts and the services which they provide.

The first task must be to look at the terminology which is commonly used to analyse and classify currency risk and to find the most useful definitions for such expressions as economic, transaction, accounting and translation risk. That is the subject of Part 1.

We distinguish first between economic and financial risk. We define economic risk as the threat that the costs of a business might become uncompetitive because the real purchasing power of its currency has risen to a point where competitors with costs in other currencies have gained a significant advantage. This is clearly what happened to companies with sterling costs in the years 1977 to 1980. Having defined this as economic risk, we then define all other risks as financial risks, and this includes the risks that most people have in mind when they talk about currency risks. Financial risks can lead to losses realized in cash, or unrealized losses which show up in companies' financial statements.

Financial risks are then subdivided into *trading risks*, which arise from selling in currencies other than those of cost, and *balance sheet risks*, which arise from having either more or less assets than liabilities

1

in any given currency other than the currency in which we measure our gains and losses—in most cases our reporting currency.

The remainder of the book is concerned with the problems of trading and balance sheet risk. In Part 2 we look at the environmental topics of the causes of currency movements and accounting conventions. In Part 3 we look at the tools of risk management, in Part 4 at the problems of managing trading risks, in Part 5 at the complex puzzle of fully describing balance sheet risk and the difference between the 'true' and the accounting view of that risk, and in Part 6 we examine the problems of managing balance sheet risk. Finally in Part 7 we cease to look at the topic as it faces a treasurer, and take the bird's-eye view of the main board of directors, and describe their task of formulating attitudes, objectives, policies, and then rules and disciplines for the management of financial currency risk. We do not do this for economic currency risk because we find that this is part of a wider corporate planning task which lies outside the scope of this book.

Currency risk and its management is riddled with conflicts which need to be resolved. In the field of trading risk there can be a dilemma between avoiding risk and getting orders. We can sometimes harmonize these objectives, but at other times, especially when a company must tender for a large contract in a currency which is not that of cost, we cannot. Another possible conflict is between accounting and true risk. A company can take much trouble to balance its assets and liabilities in all currencies, only to find that when it needs to dispose of a major asset, this very effort to balance out all the accounting exposures has created an actual cash currency loss on that disposal. Another possible conflict is between looking at a risk only as far as the next annual reporting date and looking at it for its expected life-span; we shall find that this dilemma is easily resolved. There can be a conflict between avoiding balance sheet risk and financing the company or group at the lowest cost in interest rates. There can also be a conflict between the needs of a group of companies and the interests of the individual member companies in the group. There is an obvious dilemma between the considerable resources that may be needed to control and manage currency risk and the need to save overhead costs in competitive business. And an even more important choice is between defensive and aggressive attitudes to currency risk. Are we trying to avoid loss? Or are we concerned to take well-judged exposures and make money out of currencies? To put it another way, are we here to make money out of making and marketing, say, toys, or are we here simply to make money for our stockholders out of any activity or opportunity, including currency movements?

This last question is not, of course, for this book to answer. Every company must answer it for itself. But we do suggest in this book that if a company wishes to manage currencies for profit, it may find it rewarding and cost-effective to manage its normal operating risks defensively, and to take deliberate open risks on battlegrounds of its own choosing. This strategy might win some larger gains with much less effort than it would take to get similar results in the jungle of numerous unselected operating exposures.

Our point of departure in this book is that every company needs a capability to manage risks at a zero level. This can be achieved by a rule-book which lays this down as the norm. Most companies will then wish to take controlled deviations from this zero risk position, under the safeguard of clearly established delegated authority levels. These would also be laid down in the rule-book. Risks can be authorized by category, and this management structure for the approval of risk does not have to be cumbersome.

One of the most controversial conclusions reached in this enquiry is that currency expertise must be fed into *pricing decisions* where it is proposed to sell in a currency which is not that of the costs. The decision process involves not only the acceptance of that mismatch, but also the use of a particular exchange rate at which the price desired in the currency of cost is converted into a selling price in another currency. There is an implied judgement that when we ultimately come to sell the currency of the price for the currency of cost, the dealing rate will be no less favourable than the rate we used to arrive at our price. However, it could in fact turn out to be less favourable and result in a currency loss. The controversial conclusion reached in this book is that currency expertise is needed for this aspect of the pricing decision process, and will be needed again as soon as the sale becomes a commercial or contractual fact, because at that time the foreign currency price should be sold forward or at any rate hedged by some available hedging tool. The two events can of course occur simultaneously. We are suggesting an interface between the treasurer and the commercial manager who sets prices. This interface is of course needed only where we are to quote a price in a currency which is not that of cost. It takes no special currency expertise to match the currency of price and of cost. But where we do need such an interface, this cuts across many conventional ideas of organization structures. Again, it is unlikely that this suggestion will normally be burdensome to implement, as in most businesses there are rather less pricing decisions to be made than might be thought. For example a single decision to issue a price list can set the prices for very large numbers of individual sales transactions.

Our review of balance sheet risk finds that conflicts between the accounting and the true view of that risk are gradually being narrowed. The main sources of conflict would disappear if current value accounting became universal, especially for fixed assets, and if accounting standards permitted the full offsetting of deliberately balanced positions in each currency.

We find that the worst problem in the management of balance sheet risk is the timing problem, in other words, the need to look for the most profitable time to execute each deal in the currency markets, whenever we have failed to avoid or hedge an exposure at its inception.

But balance sheet risks, for all their greater complexity, have the saving grace that their management is part of the wider problem of financing the company or group. Generally, therefore, the task involves only the corporate financial management team, and no difficult interfaces with commercial or other functions, whose approach to risk may be less cautious and prudent by the very nature of their tasks.

These are the fundamental patterns which we discover as we survey the field in detail.

PART 1

Definitions and Fundamentals

CHAPTER 2

What is so Difficult about Defining Currency Risk?

The business world has little doubt about the existence of currency risks. It is widely known that J. Lyons of teashop fame had to sell their teashops and lost their independence because they borrowed non-sterling currencies to finance assets in the United Kingdom, and that Rolls Royce recorded a very large loss in 1979 because they had taken major contracts in US dollars.

It is also generally understood that the problem has been at least greatly aggravated since currencies began to float in 1971. Currencies have fluctuated quite sharply, and this can cause very large gains or losses if the risks are not avoided or managed.

But there seems to be rather less agreement on just what is a currency risk. Books on this subject use a number of expressions like economic, transaction, accounting, translation, balance sheet exposures, but they do not all define them in the same way, and very few authors have set out rigorous or formal definitions.

One author who does define exposures formally, is David P. Walker (1978). He says that 'an asset, liability or income-stream is exposed to exchange risk when a currency movement will change, for better or worse, its parent currency value'. He defines an *accounting* exposure as 'the possibility that those foreign currency-denominated items which are consolidated into a company's published financial statements will show a translation loss (or gain) as a result of currency movements since the previous balance-sheet date'. He also defines *economic* exposure as 'the possibility that the parent currency-denominated net present value of the foreign subsidiary's cash flows will be adversely affected by exchange rate movements'.

Andreas Prindl (1976) defines *accounting* risk as the possibility 'that the publicly stated value of the company's assets, equity and income may be adversely affected by the movement of currencies in which it has dealings'. His view of *economic* exposure takes in 'the whole range of the *future* effects of parity changes which have occurred or may possibly occur in the future'. It includes the case 'where an actual conversion may be made or where the cash flow effect of an exchange loss is an impediment to the operations of one subsidiary', but also 'the impact on future sales of a company situated in a country whose currency has appreciated, or on future profits where the local currency has depreciated'. He goes on to say that 'the impact of actual conversions is called "*transaction exposure*" but this is not as all-encompassing as the term "*economic exposure*" '.

John Heywood (1978) defines *balance sheet* or *translation* exposure much as David Walker defines accounting exposure. On the other hand, for *economic* or *transaction* exposure he quotes the simplest case where a company has 'one export order to sell goods in currency: if the currency in which the goods are invoiced appreciates, the company will make a gain, if it depreciates, the company will suffer a loss'. He adds however that 'the exposure arises as soon as the order is taken, but it will not show in the financial accounts . . . until it becomes a "receivable" '.

J. A. Donaldson (1980) distinguishes between *transaction* and *translation* exposures. *Transaction* exposures 'are revenue in nature and exist for relatively short periods'. He says that a sale from seller to buyer in another country must be in the currency of at best one of them, and the other one has an exposure, but only 'when there is a period of delay in payment for the goods' and 'most transaction exposures arise from the granting of credit'. *Translation* exposures, on the other hand 'relate to the balance sheet and are in existence for periods in excess of a year'.

These examples illustrate that the terminology is not yet agreed. There is some similarity of views about balance sheet, translation and accounting risk, which most authors treat as almost interchangeable terms.

Some authors identify the quite separate risks (a) where the proceeds of a sale are converted at a loss because the exchange rate has moved adversely, and (b) where the costs of a business have risen against those of competitors, due to a rise in the 'real' (inflation-corrected) exchange rate of its currency, and where this adverse shift in its competitive cost structure threatens its market share and margins. But some call both of these 'economic' risk, some reserve the term for the first of them and some for the last. Some do not consider the risk to comparative costs at all. The term 'transaction' exposure is used by Donaldson to describe the loss from realizing a worse exchange rate at the end of a trading transaction, and by Prindl as one of the economic risks and by way of contrast apparently with the case where a loss is sustained without an actual exchange conversion.

But if these matters are still without even a broadly agreed set of definitions, there are other aspects which need to be resolved before we can really chart the field of currency risk with the aid of a reasonably precise terminology:

* When does exposure begin, and when does it end?
* What are the amounts exposed to risk?
* What is the base exchange rate from which deviations cause risk?

* Is the risk always measured in the parent reporting currency?
* Are the expressions balance sheet risk, accounting or translation risk interchangeable terms, and are they incompatible with the concept of a transaction risk? Can there be such a thing as an accounting or translation risk in respect of a trading transaction?
* Do balance sheet gains and losses arise only at reporting dates?
* And do they arise only in the process of consolidating the accounts of the various companies in a group?

The next four chapters are devoted to an attempt to answer these questions and to set out a cohesive conceptual framework for the field of currency risks and their management.

References

Donaldson, J. A. (1980), *Corporate Currency Risk*, The Financial Times Business Information Ltd., London, p. 8.

Heywood, J. (1978), *Foreign Exchange and the Corporate Treasurer*, Black, London, pp. 53–54 and 66.

Prindl, A. R. (1976), *Foreign Exchange Risk*, Wiley, London, p. 21.

Walker, D. P. (1978), 'An economic analysis of foreign exchange risk', Research Committee Occasional Paper No. 14, Institute of Chartered Accountants in England and Wales, pp. 6 and 30.

CHAPTER 3

The Definition of Economic Currency Risk

A good starting point is David Walker's (1978) definition of economic risk, which is also one of the two categories of economic risk in Andreas' Prindl's (1976) definition.

A Swiss company makes and sells goods in its own and other markets. Its principal competitor is in Holland. The inflation rate is 5% in Holland and nil in Switzerland, but the Swiss franc rises against the Dutch guilder at the rate of $10\frac{1}{4}$% annually. As $\frac{110.25}{105}$ = 1.05, the Swiss company's comparative real (that is, inflation-adjusted) costs therefore rise by 5% per annum against those of its competitor, purely as a result of the real rise of the Swiss franc against the guilder at the rate of 5% annually. At first only the margins of the Swiss company may shrink, but in the long run it will not be able to take the whole strain on its margins, and its sales and market share will suffer. Nor will this loss of market share be confined to its export markets, but will spread to the Swiss market which comes to find the Dutch product cheaper (we are assuming that the Swiss company cannot improve its efficiency more than the Dutch company can). This experience was of course a common one among UK manufacturing companies when sterling rose in real terms in 1977–80.

What we are describing is clearly a currency risk. Its distinguishing characteristics are:

* it is the consequence of movements in real (inflation-corrected) exchange rates;
* it is environmental, occurring irrespective of the currency in which the company *sells*; it affects any one sale before it ever occurs, not because an exchange rate has moved after a price has been quoted or after a balance sheet-date;
* its consequences may not be identifiable in the financial statements; for example, its result may be to prevent some sales altogether.

All other currency risks can in some way at least be described in terms of their effect on the company's financial statements, even if that is not how we actually define some of them. They exist in the same dimension as financial reporting. They result in financial gains and losses. The risk which we are here describing on the other hand hits the comparative costs of a business and therefore its ability to book certain sales at all. The missing sales will of course have financial effects, such as unrecovered overhead. But the risks are essentially economic rather than financial.

These two concepts of risk are so fundamentally different that we do well to follow David Walker in giving these risks a separate name and restricting the expression 'economic currency risk' to them. Moreover, as all other kinds of currency risk have a common characteristic, it is helpful to find a collective definition for all the others, and call them 'financial' currency risks. Economic currency risks, as we have now identified them, have a very wide range of impact on businesses. They can for example hit a business which neither imports nor exports and has no foreign operations. Thus a restaurant or public house can lose some of its holiday trade when its home currency gets so strong as to discourage foreign tourists.

A formal definition of economic currency risk would then describe it as the risk that a sustained real rise of a currency against the currencies of competitors will adversely affect a company's competitive costs, and therefore its sales, profit margins and market share, which in turn will reduce the return on the capital and revenue investment previously sunk in its present commercial activity, and the present value of that investment.

Having defined economic currency risk, we can now tackle the various forms of financial risk in subsequent chapters.

References

Prindl, A. R. (1976). *Foreign Exchange Risk*, Wiley, London, p. 21.
Walker, D. P. (1978). 'An economic analysis of foreign exchange risk', Research Committee Occasional Paper No. 14, Institute of Chartered Accountants in England and Wales, pp. 6 and 20.

CHAPTER 4

Definition of Trading Risk

In the previous chapter we distinguished economic risks from all those which cause financial gains or losses, which we decided should collectively be called 'financial' risks. The remaining risks which we described in Chapter 2 in fact fall into two categories, those which various authors call balance sheet or accounting or translation risks, and those where, as John Heywood (1978) puts it, a company 'has one export order to sell goods in currency: if the currency ... appreciates, the company will make a gain, if it depreciates, the company will suffer a loss'. We shall call the former 'balance sheet risks' (see Chapter 5) and the latter 'trading risks'.

Examples 1 and 2

The business of a company in the United Kingdom is importing and exporting. It exports in US dollars. It has accepted orders on the assumption that the £/$ rate will be no worse than $2 = £1 when it comes to collect the dollars and converts them into sterling. Its plan for a typical consignment is to purchase the goods for £400, incur sterling overhead and selling expense of £60, make a profit of £40, and realize the total of £500 by selling at a price of $1000. If now the dollar falls against sterling by one-third, the result will look as follows:

Example 1

	Planned $2 = £1 £	Actual $3 = £1 £	Currency effect £
Price $1000	500	333	(167)
Purchase cost £400	400	400	–
selling overhead £60	60	60	–
total cost	460	460	–
profit/(loss)	40	(127)	(167)

Example 2

Here the only change is that we assume the purchase cost to be fixed in dollars at $800, and paid after the fall in the dollar:

Price $1000	500	333	(167)
Purchase cost $800	400	267	133
selling overhead £60	60	60	–
total cost	460	327	133
profit/(loss)	40	6	(34)

In Example 1 all the costs and profit were in sterling, so that the entire price was at risk. The currency loss was therefore a third of £500 = £167. In Example 2 only the selling overhead and profit of (£60 + £40) = £100 were in sterling and exposed against the dollar price, so that the currency loss was a third of £100 = (rounded) £34.

Examples 1 and 2 illustrate the nature of trading risk and its distinctive features:

* The cause of the risk is the mismatch between the currency of price and the currency of cost. For this purpose we treat the profit as a cost element: this is discussed below. In Example 1 the mismatch is the whole £500, and in Example 2 only £100.
* The amount of the risk is the amount of the mismatch.
* The gain or loss is caused by the difference between the planned exchange rate used in the *pricing decision* and the exchange rate actually realized in cash when the sale proceeds are converted into the currency of cost. The gain or loss is the difference between the amount at risk converted (a) at the planned rate, and (b) at the actually realized rate.
* Timing of exchange deals is important if we want to net items in the currency from which we need to convert. In Example 2 we could not have reduced the amount at risk by the $800 purchase cost if we had bought that $800 for sterling before the dollar fell from $2 to $3 per pound sterling.

We assumed that the risk had crystallized when the selling price was established at $1000. This would obviously not have been so if the currencies of cost had not at that stage been known. If at that time all the costs could still have been fixed in dollars, the exposure might still have been avoided.

We also treated the *profit* as if it were a sterling *cost* element. Sterling was after all not only our reporting currency, but also the currency into which we converted our dollar proceeds (in Example 2 our net dollar proceeds after paying our dollar costs). But if the sale had occurred in our US subsidiary, and if all costs and the price had been fixed in dollars, then we should have regarded the trading exposure as wholly avoided. For in that case the planned profit would have been a dollar profit too;

it would have been protected, and the dollar is the local company's functional or reporting currency. But from the point of view of the UK parent company that profit is a dollar risk which our definition of balance sheet risk in Chapters 20 and 21 clearly accommodates within that concept. But the act of matching currency of cost with currency of price has ensured the preservation of that profit as a positive item. The parent company's balance sheet risk cannot turn it into a loss. Example 13 in Chapter 13 (page 69) illustrates the order of magnitude.

Formal definition

Trading currency risk can therefore be defined as the risk of not achieving the planned profit margin on sales where the selling price and the costs are not in the same currency, due to an adverse movement in the exchange rate from the rate used in the pricing decision, between the time of that decision and the receipt of payment. The necessary elements are the currency mismatch and the time-lag between the pricing decision and the collection of the payment, which constitutes the opportunity to convert the currency received into the currency of cost.

Purchase price decisions

It is not always the *selling* price decision which crystallizes the base exchange rate against which there is an exposure. For example if a French company, which incurs all its costs and sells all its products in its domestic currency, commissions a major consultancy report for which it must pay a large sum in US dollars, it quite evidently incurs a risk on the dollar from the moment it takes the dollar *purchase decision*. It used some rate of exchange to evaluate the cost in French francs. When it comes to pay the dollars at some other exchange rate, it stands to make a currency gain or loss on the difference between the two rates. In that case the vital pricing decision was the purchasing decision. In fact, in many companies the exposure on purchasing in other currencies receives far less attention than the decision to sell in other currencies. And yet in the case of a capital expenditure project the entire economics of the investment appraisal could be upset by a significant currency movement in the cost.

Netting price with cost: the synchronization problem

We noted that in Example 2 the risk would not be reduced to the net $200 = £100 if the $800 purchase cost were paid by conversion from sterling *before* the dollar price was received and at a different exchange rate. In practice this can be avoided by using a bank account in dollars, which can be overdrawn if the costs are paid first and then reimbursed from the sale proceeds before the balance of $200 is converted into sterling, provided of course that there are no exchange control obstacles to this procedure.

Trading risks become balance sheet items

The sales and purchases are likely to turn up on the balance sheet as receivables and payables. Whether this turns them into balance sheet risks, is discussed in Chapter 19.

Trading risks as accounting risks

In Chapter 2 we quoted Prindl's (1976) use of the expression 'transaction' risk for a trading risk which is realized as a cash gain or loss. 'Transaction' risk is contrasted with 'accounting' or 'translation' risk. 'Accounting' gains or losses are unrealized, and appear in the process of translating assets and liabilities into the reporting currencies when a balance sheet is prepared, or into the parent reporting currency when a consolidated balance sheet is prepared. Such assets and liabilities would of course include receivables and payables. Chapter 6 deals with the difference between accounting and transaction risk, but we must here note that it would be quite wrong to identify trading risks as we have defined them with transaction risks, and to think that they can never turn up as accounting (or translation) exposures. A trading risk begins with the pricing decision and ends with the cash conversion; between those two events there may well be one or even several annual accounting dates (especially in construction projects or where long-term credit is involved), at which the trading item may feature in the balance sheet as inventory, receivable or payable, and the translation of the items may well be at the spot rate on the date of the balance sheet. This would normally show a *provisional* gain or loss from the currency risk, which is likely to differ from the final cash or 'transaction' outcome. We must therefore note here that trading risks can and often do involve accounting exposures, before discussing the whole issue fully in Chapter 6.

Technical note on currency escalation clauses

Sometimes, often for exchange control reasons, contracts of sale specify that the price is remittable in one currency, but is effectively determined in another. For example 'the price is £1100 sterling, but all variations from $2.20 = £1 are for the purchaser's account'. In that case the price is effectively fixed at $2420 and the US supplier has no risk against his dollar costs; that risk is firmly placed with the customer in the United Kingdom. The clause can have other effects too. For example, under the exchange control regulations in force in the United Kingdom until 1979, the purchaser resident in the United Kingdom could not have covered the payment forward because it was a payment in sterling. One variety of these currency adjustment clauses leaves a margin such as the first ±1% variation (that is, between $2.178 and $2.222) at the seller's, and only the excess at the purchaser's risk. This still leaves the *open-ended* risk with the UK customer.

Reference

Heywood, J. (1978), *Foreign Exchange and the Corporate Treasurer*, Black, London.
Prindl, A. (1976), *Foreign Exchange Risk*, Wiley, London, p. 21.

CHAPTER 5

Balance Sheet Risks

We have so far identified a main classification between economic and financial risks, and a subclassification of financial risk into trading risks and balance sheet risks. We found that trading risks involve a currency mismatch between currency of cost and currency of price, and a picture is emerging that balance sheet risk involves something similar, but between assets and liabilities. We shall find balance sheet risk more difficult to define, and in this chapter we shall only be able to reach provisional conclusions.

When companies prepare financial statements, all balance sheet items which are not carried in the reporting currency, must nevertheless be shown in that currency, or rather 'translated' into it. Strictly, this involves two distinct operations. First, in each individual company: the Swedish subsidiary of a German company may have items in D-marks, sterling and lire on its balance sheet, all of which it must translate into Swedish kronor in order to prepare its own accounts. Secondly, if the German parent company prepares consolidated accounts, it will have to 'translate' the balance sheet of the Swedish company into D-marks.

It seems to be clear to all writers that if the exchange rates between the four currencies in this example have moved between the last two balance sheet dates, exchange differences will appear which constitute some currency gains or losses. Clearly in the preparation of the Swedish company's accounts they arise against the Swedish krona, and in the consolidation against the D-mark. Clearly also the balance sheet risk arises in both processes, preparing the accounts of a single company and consolidating the accounts of a group.

But this leaves many other questions about the beginning and end of a risk, its quantification, whether we can have transaction risks in this balance sheet field, or whether the risk is purely an accounting phenomenon, about the impact of different accounting conventions, and about the borderline between trading and balance sheet exposure. We asked most of these questions at the end of Chapter 2.

Much of the literature on this subject is preoccupied with the accounting conventions in force in various countries from time to time. This is natural because the accounting standard setting bodies are themselves searching for further improvements in this field. Some writers go to the length of defining all balance sheet risk as 'translation' risk. We can accept 'translation' and 'accounting' risk as interchangeable expressions in this context; after all, translation is one of the processes in preparing accounts. But the writers who define all balance sheet risk as 'translation' risk seem to imply that there is no such thing as a risk in this field which would arise even if we did not prepare accounts, or which could not result in a gain or loss at a time when we do not happen to be preparing accounts. We shall look at the accounting conventions in Chapter 8. In Chapter 6, we shall examine in depth whether in the field of balance sheets it makes sense to speak of 'transaction' exposure. In this chapter we are having a first look at some of the other questions.

Examples 3, 4 and 5 below show in simple form how an excess of assets over liabilities, or an excess of liabilities over assets, in any currency other than the parent reporting currency constitutes an exposure to changes in the rates between the other currencies and the parent currency.

The examples deal with monetary assets and liabilities only. This avoids all controversy about accounting conventions, and the losses will strike the plain man as 'true', if unrealized. For if they had been realized on the closing date, the cash losses would have been those shown in the examples. And we are showing the currency losses on one line, without enquiring whether the reported profit or loss is affected. We do this in Chapter 8.

Although the examples show losses which arise in a single company, it is easy to see that the losses would be exactly the same if we had been looking at a consolidated balance sheet in which the assets were held indirectly through a wholly owned subsidiary company.

Examples 3, 4 and 5

A German company produces its accounts in D-marks. The company is during the period of the example dormant; it has no income and incurs no expense. During this period its debt and deposits are assumed to be interest-free for the purpose of this illustration. In Example 3 its sole asset is DM1000 worth of dollar deposit, financed by DM1000 share capital. In Example 4 that same dollar deposit is financed by DM200 share capital and DM800 worth of dollar borrowing. In example 5 a D-mark deposit of DM1000 is financed by DM200 share capital and DM800 worth of Swiss franc debt.

Opening balance sheets in DM: $1 = DM 2 = Sw Fr 2

	Example 3	Example 4	Example 5
DM share capital	1000	200	200
dollar debt	–	800	–
Sw Fr debt	–	–	800
Funds employed	1000	1000	1000

Asset

Dollar deposit	1000	1000	

DM deposit			1000

By the end of the period the exchange rates had moved to a closing position of $1 = DM 1.75 = Sw Fr 1.50.

Closing balance sheets in DM

DM share capital	1000	200	200
currency loss	(125)	(25)	(133)
dollar debt	–	700	–
Sw Fr debt	–	–	933
Funds employed	875	875	1000

Asset

Dollar deposit	875	875	

DM deposit			1000

The currency losses are:

In Example 3: one-eighth of DM1000 because the dollar has fallen against the D-mark by one-eighth.

In Example 4: one-eighth of DM200, because the unmatched asset was only DM1000 – DM800.

In Example 5: one-sixth of DM800, because the D-mark has fallen against the Swiss franc by one-sixth.

A small extension of the examples will also show us the interesting point that the exposure consists not of any individual asset or liability, but of the net total of assets less liabilities in a given currency. For if in Example 5 the assets had consisted of four current account balances owed by four other companies, one of DM400 and three of DM200 each, the exposure and the currency loss to the net worth of the German company would have been unaffected, just as it would not have made any difference if the Swiss franc liability had consisted of several such balances totalling Sw Fr800. The exposure is a net global one. This is different from the case of trading risks, where each separate pricing decision creates a separate risk. One pricing decision, like the one that goes into a price list, can of course give rise to thousands of transactions which constitute a single exposure, but it would not be correct for example to regard all sales in lire which occur in a particular period as a single exposure, unless they all involved a single pricing decision. When on the other hand we look at balance sheet risks, the amount at risk is the net total of all assets and liabilities in any one currency, taken collectively. This net balance will in most businesses fluctuate continually, and the risk management implications of this continual change are considered in Chapter 23. But at any one point in time that net total constitutes the extent to which the net worth of the group or company is at risk.

The three examples do not tell us anything about the time at which risk begins or ends. In the example we have taken the *opening* date as the beginning, and the opening rates as the base exchange rates against which gains or losses are calculated, but this is simply because the examples gave us no other information to use. Again, this difficult point is developed in Chapter 20. But we can note that if in Example 5 the Swiss franc debt and the bulk of the D-mark deposit had come into being in the middle of the period, the risk would have begun then, and the base exchange rate would have been the one at which the francs then borrowed would have been converted to produce D-marks on that date.

First shot at defining balance sheet risk

In these simplified terms, then, we can now set out a first provisional definition of balance sheet risk as the risk of loss to the net worth of the company or group from movements in the parity of the parent currency against any currency in which the group or company has an imbalance of assets and liabilities. It is that imbalance without which there would be no risk. Nor could there be a risk where there is no time-lag during which currencies have an opportunity to move.

CHAPTER 6

Transaction versus Accounting Risk

At the end of Chapter 4 we noticed that trading risks can be accounting (= translation) risks. For between the time that a company commits itself to a price unmatched in currency with its costs, and the time that the transaction is realized in cash so that receipts and costs come together in a single currency, there may well be one or more annual reporting dates at which the balances resulting from the transaction have to be translated into the reporting currency and thus show a currency gain or loss. This gain or loss is an unrealized provisional loss. It is an accounting or translation loss, not a cash or transaction loss. And if for any reason the company wishes to manage the risk *with an eye on* the reporting date, rather than on the final cash outcome of the exposure, then it is managing the risk as an accounting risk, not as a transaction risk. The underlying risk is the same; whether we manage or view it as an account- ing or as a transaction risk is an important distinction, but it is *in the eye of the beholder.*

It is therefore worth looking at balance sheet risks, to see whether they too can be looked at and managed either as accounting or as trans- action risks. It is in fact quite easy to construct an example where a balance sheet risk shows all the same relevant characteristics as a trad- ing risk.

Example 6

A company in Holland appoints a new Canadian distributor, and agrees to grant that distributor a start-up loan of Canadian $200 000, repayable in full after 2 years. The company has the option of borrowing Canadian $200 000 to finance this loan, in which case it is not opening up a new risk on the Canadian dollar. Alternatively if it does not borrow the matching currency, then it has a new exposure of Canadian $200 000 with a definite maturity date. It is likely that between the birth of this risk when the advance takes place, and its death 2 years later when it is repaid, there will be two annual reporting dates, at which the balance in Canadian dollars will be translated into guilders, which is the reporting currency. The company is free to view and manage this risk as an accounting risk if it so wishes. But essentially the risk is also a transaction risk because at maturity the Canadian $200 000 will be repaid and the company is free to sell them for guilders and thus crystallize in cash a transaction gain or loss. The figures work out as follows:

Year		Event	Rate	Amount in Dfl
1	15 March	Loan advanced	1.60	320 000
1	30 June	Annual accounts	1.80	360 000
2	30 June	Annual accounts	1.70	340 000
3	15 March	Loan repaid	1.55	310 000

The original cost of the Canadian $200 000 was Dfl320 000. The amount finally received back in guilders was Dfl310 000. So there was an overall transaction loss of Dfl10 000. But at the first annual reporting date the translation showed a gain of Dfl40 000. The next annual accounts showed a loss for that year of Dfl20 000 (a cumulative gain reduced from Dfl40 000 to Dfl20 000), and the annual accounts for 30 June in year 3 showed a loss realized *in that year* of Dfl30 000.

It is interesting to note that the example would show exactly the same currency gains and losses if the Dutch company, instead of making a loan, had sold goods at a price of Canadian $200 000 with a credit period of 2 years and a planned guilder price of Dfl320 000. From the point of view of understanding the difference between trading and balance sheet risk, it is important that the trading risk version involves a pricing decision with the rate of Dfl1.60 = Canadian $1 built into the decision, whereas the balance sheet risk begins with an actual spot exchange transaction at that rate. But from the point of view of the difference between accounting and transaction risk, it is immaterial whether we are here looking at a commercial sale or a lending transaction. For in both cases we have a monetary asset of Canadian $200 000 on our balance sheet, either a loan or a receivable, and in both cases we have the same definite maturity date.

The example clearly shows that there is nothing mutually exclusive about the concepts of balance sheet risk and transaction risk. The company can, if it takes that view, look upon its risk as beginning with the advance and ending with the repayment of the loan 2 years later, and for example avoid it altogether by borrowing the Canadian dollars for precisely that period. And such a borrowing of Canadian dollars would equally avoid the alternative trading risk (if the dollar asset had been a receivable instead of a loan), *provided* that we managed to sell the original proceeds of the borrowing at the rate of Dfl1.60 for the planned price of Dfl320 000.

Alternatively the company could of course take the view that it is only concerned with the effect in its accounts, and will therefore manage the risk with an eye only on the next balance sheet date. Many companies take that view. In that case it might borrow the Canadian $200 000 only for the period 15 March to 1 July in year 1. It is then safe against showing any loss (or gain) in its accounts at 30 June due to any movement in the Canadian dollar. But what will the company do on 1 July? If it manages to extend the loan either to 15 March in year 3 or to 1 July in year 2 (followed by a further extension to 15 March in year 3), then a loss or gain will have been avoided in all the financial statements and on final cash realization. We are ignoring the effect on interest here, which is dealt with in Chapter 21.

Similarly, if the company had sold the Canadian dollars forward on 15 March in year 1 to 15 March in year 3 (forward cover is described in chapter 9), it would have fixed the guilder value of the loan for *all three* forward dates (the two reporting dates and the final repayment date), whereas a forward contract to 1 July in year 1 would merely have fixed the guilder value up to that date.

The example shows that there can be such a thing as a transaction exposure in balance sheet risks, and that where we have this phenomenon there is at first sight much to be said for treating it as a transaction risk. This is particularly so if we wish to manage these risks defensively so as to avoid loss.

We should note that the concept of a currency imbalance on the balance sheet as a transaction risk is relatively easy to see where the imbalance consists of *monetary* items, as in the example. It would evidently be more difficult with fixed assets. But this view of balance sheet risks as transaction risks does raise problems. The concept of transaction risk seems to involve the concept of a definite cash maturity, and this gives rise to the following difficulties:

1. We found in chapter 5 that balance sheet risk concerns not individual assets and liabilities, but the net total balance in any one currency other than the reporting currency.
2. Fixed assets have no predetermined maturities or lives. Their balance sheet value declines with depreciation. At the unknown end of their lives there is not necessarily a significant cash realization.
3. The purchase of a new foreign subsidiary may look to the parent like a single long-term asset. In later chapters we shall describe this view as the island theory or the net investment concept. The newly acquired subsidiary may contain some short-life assets like receivables maturing this coming week, but to the new parent company all this looks like one single, perpetually self-renewing investment. The currency composition of the risk and its overall size will of course fluctuate with seasons, with changes in customer mix, product mix and currency mix. Is all this a single currency risk or a multitude of different categories and maturities?

There are two underlying issues of principle. One is the valuation of the risks. If we look at them in accounting terms, we can get a picture which can, under some accounting conventions, sharply vary from its true value to the parent company. That dilemma is described in Chapter 8, and in Chapter 21 we try to resolve it. The second of the two issues is that of the *time horizon*. This we cannot finally tackle until we have had a more detailed look at the tools and problems of managing currency risks.

But on this issue of the time horizon we can even at this stage form one preliminary conclusion. In fact we can quite firmly note that whenever we know that a risk will have a life-span beyond the date of the next balance sheet date, and if we are concerned to avoid loss, we should not restrict our view to that reporting date. We may not have an accurate view of that life, but we do in many cases know that it will continue beyond the next 9 months, possibly many years more. In that case in managing that risk we should put some duration, even if it has to be arbitrary, on the life of that risk, and aim to deal with it for the duration of that assumed life-span. And we can be quite firm about this, because in these terms we have no practical dilemma to face. We want to approach this risk either aggressively, that is, accept it with a view to making a gain from it, or defensively, that is, avoid or hedge it so as to avoid loss. In the former case we are not concerned with the time horizon anyway. In the latter case we shall probably wish to neutralize the risk by a borrowing in the same currency (assuming the risk to be positive, that is, assets in the currency exceed liabilities) or by forward cover or by some other device discussed in Chapters 9 to 11. And here we have already found that if we succeed in hedging the risk for its entire life-span, we shall automatically also hedge it for all the intervening reporting dates. This discovery does not of course tell us how to *value* the risk, in other words, whether to measure it in accounting terms or 'true' terms, but we can safely decide that the exposure should not be regarded as having a life ending on the date of the next annual accounts of the company or group.

We have therefore reached a very important set of conclusions, which is central to an insight into the nature of currency risk.

* All financial risks, that is, not only trading risks but also balance sheet risks, can be viewed and managed as transaction risks.
* Where the choice arises, that is, for all risks which we know will continue beyond the next balance sheet date, the practical view is to look at them as transaction rather than accounting risks.

Many people will baulk at the very concept of a transaction balance sheet risk. It sounds semantically like a contradiction in terms, because we think of the word 'transaction' more readily in a revenue than a capital context. We also tend to be conscious of the fact that the end of the life of a non-monetary asset is not easily seen as a kind of cash disposal, which is the picture conjured up by the word 'transaction'. Finally, many of us inherit rather than start balance sheet risks; they tend to have grown naturally in the Bretton Woods era or before. This too makes it hard for us to see them as 'transactions'. All these points are understandable, some of them even objectively correct. But they must not be permitted to lead us to the conclusion that balance sheet risks should be viewed and managed as accounting risks, with a mental horizon at the next reporting date.

PART 2

The Floating Currency and Accounting Background

CHAPTER 7

Can we Forecast Exchange Rates?

The question of how predictable currency movements are is obviously a key issue in the field of currency risk management. If rates are predictable within acceptable margins of error, the management of currency risk would have to look no further.

Fig. 1 shows a graph of the average monthly value of the dollar/sterling spot rate over some years. The fluctuations are seen to be heavy, with sharp reversals of trend. From $2.419 in March 1975 the rate took 20 months to fall by 32.3% to $1.637 in November 1976; 23 months later it had climbed back 22.6% to $2.007, and by October 1980 it had attained the March 1975 average again.

Those swings in the monthly average values understate the volatility of this spot rate, which can easily move by as much as 3% in a few hours of one afternoon's trading.

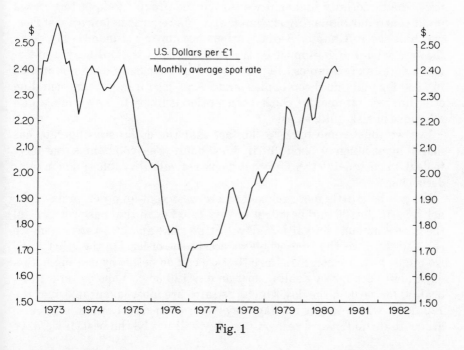

Fig. 1

29

What are acceptable margins of error in forecasting?

Having established that currencies are volatile, we must turn to how much volatility a treasurer can live with. In this discussion we shall have to anticipate some technical points like forward cover, which is described in Chapter 9.

Currency risk management involves a number of different kinds of risk: for example, balance sheet risks, ordinary trading risks and large contract trading risks. It also involves a great variety of companies with different attitudes to currency risk (ranging from aggressive to defensive) and different situations; for example, are we trying to predict the precise spot rate at which we can sell a foreign currency receipt 12 months from now, or the rates at which we can sell forward our receipts over 5 years, when in 9 months' time we may receive an order for that contract? Are we trying to predict a particular rate at all? Or are we trying to assess merely whether the spot rate will be better for us to deal at than the forward rate available now? Or are we trying to judge whether the best time to cover forward an existing exposure is now, or whether a more favourable opportunity may occur during the rest of the life of the particular exposure?

What is an acceptable margin of error evidently depends on many factors. If the error becomes a gain or a loss to the trading profits of a small subsidiary, the acceptable level is likely to be low, whereas it might be materially higher if we turned the group headquarters into a profit centre for managing exchange risk. As regards balance sheet risk, we shall see in Chapter 8 that various accounting standards lay down that *every* gain or loss must be treated as part of the ordinary profit or loss before tax (examples are the US and UK exposure drafts published in 1980 for individual companies, and FAS 8 for all reporting, including consolidated statements). Such a convention is likely to make companies' tolerance of risk quite small.

But we must come back to the fact that the dollar/sterling rate has moved by as much as about 3% in a few hours. Few companies that have to deal on such a day can find that degree of volatility tolerable for their decisions.

We can be a little more relaxed where we accept an order on day 1 for delivery on day 30 and payment on day 120. For in that case we can sell the entire amount forward on day 1 at no risk, and at a rate which we can determine at the time when we accept the order. On the other hand we might have reason to believe that we can do better by dealing not on day 1, but perhaps by dealing spot on day 120 or perhaps better still by dealing forward on the day which the rates are most favourable over the 120 days, which might be (say) day 47. But on day 1 we only have to decide that the forward rate on that day will not be the best. If we have

good and well-informed grounds for that judgement, it is legitimate to
act on it.

To sum up, there are many situations in which our tolerance for error
is likely to be too narrow for the market at its most volatile, and many
other situations where our need for accuracy is less critical.

What makes currencies fluctuate and move?

Whether they like it or not, companies with currency risk are in the
business of forecasting exchange rates, at least to some extent. The
causes of movements have their own specialist literature. Forecasts are
now provided by computer-based and other services. We must, however,
summarize the main factors which make currencies move, by way of
introduction and background to the problem.

Most authorities believe that currency movements are caused by some
or all the following factors which influence the demand and supply of
each currency in the markets:

* relative price-levels and inflation rates,
* relative economic growth rates,
* relative interest rates, especially in the freely traded money markets
  like the Eurocurrency market,
* relative changes in the money supply in the currency areas (countries) concerned,
* investment or portfolio preferences of big international investors,
  like the OPEC countries,
* bandwagon effects (if a currency seems to be on the way up, specu-
  lators may exaggerate the trend by buying in the hope of a quick
  profit),
* intervention by central banks.

Movements in a rate depend obviously on whether overall demand at
the existing rate is balanced by supply, and this in turn depends on the
two separate elements of the trading and capital flows across the ex-
changes. Quite often a country has a negative trade balance and a
positive capital balance or vice versa, in which case the movement of the
market depends on which countervailing imbalance is the stronger.

Of the above seven factors, the first two are likely to affect the trade
balance in the short term, and the remainder the capital balance, but in
the longer run factors like relative money supply will affect relative
economic growth, and in the really long run all these factors are likely
to become interdependent.

It is important to stress that the various causes take different time-
spans to operate. Relative prices levels are likely to have an influence in

the long run, because in the long run the laws of demand and supply will tend to equate the prices of internationally traded goods and services in all countries, if not artificially impeded by protection or exchange controls. But high interest rates may work very quickly to attract funds available for investment from one centre to another. Similarly a fast-growing money supply may encourage funds to leave the country quite quickly for investment in a centre where funds are scarcer and command a better yield.

It is instructive to reflect that those currencies in which international investment funds tend to get invested, like the US dollar, sterling, D-mark, Swiss franc and yen, are likely to have more capital transactions, than for example the Scandinavian currencies, where the trading flows are likely to predominate to a greater extent.

Central bank interventions can be massive, and are often designed to defeat the market operators who think they have a good bandwagon to climb on. It is here worth distinguishing between those interventions which one government on its own considers desirable, but may invite other central banks to support, and those which are compelled by mutual agreements between groups of governments, like the members of the European Monetary System (EMS). The latter are much more predictable than the former.

Relative interest rates are probably the most powerful short-term influence, and yet also the most unsatisfactory one from the point of view of the forecaster. Because interest levels are closely controlled by governments and central banks, they are not very capable of prediction; for at any given time the outside observer may not know how far interest rate policy is governed by domestic considerations or by the desire to keep the exchange rate up or down. Governmental motivations too are volatile.

Computer models

The volatile markets of the 1970s have caused business some considerable headaches. Hence forecasting services are springing up in response to the wish of the business community to get a better understanding of what is likely to happen. Linear equation models are at the base of many of these services. No satisfactory answers appear to have been found yet, which is hardly surprising. The various causes are not mutually independent, and they do have different and changing time-lags, and some of them, like bandwagon operations and central bank intervention, may defeat the model builder. But the development is helpful because experience is being gained in a way which can be monitored and measured, and in time our ability to use them as a forecasting tool may improve.

Other forecasting methods

More impressive results have been obtained by market analysts, sometimes called 'chartists', who study not the causes but how markets respond to them. Other forecasters concentrate on what can be gleaned about the attitudes of the people with the greatest personal influence on the demand and supply of currencies, such as the financial authorities of the major 'reserve' currencies and those responsible for administering the portfolios of the OPEC countries.

For the time being it is not safe to neglect any of these methods, as each tries to discover a different aspect of what makes rates move.

Conclusion

Our brief summary of the main issues involved in forecasting currency movements may warrant the following conclusions:

* It is doubtful whether accurate forecasting is possible in present conditions.
* All treasurers with currency exposures are unavoidably in the business of forecasting; they cannot escape the task altogether.
* They may nevertheless wish to restrict the field in which they have to forecast as much as they possibly can.

CHAPTER 8

Accounting Conventions for Currency Transactions and Currency Translation

The literature on currency risk has been much preoccupied with the accounting conventions, especially those used in both the United States and the United Kingdom.

In this book we are concerned with managing currency risk. We must therefore describe the principal accounting conventions as we find them at the end of 1980, in such detail as is important to the problems of risk management. We must then analyse what possible conflict there is between currency risk in true financial terms (not 'economic' terms; see Chapter 3) and currency risk in accounting terms, and then to assess whether or to what extent companies should concern themselves with accounting or true exposure where such conflict exists.

The most important developments in this field in the United States and the United Kingdom were:

In the United States:
* Financial Accounting Standards Board Statement No. 8 issued October 1975 (FAS 8).
* Exposure Draft for a proposed new FAS to supersede FAS 8, issued August 1980.
In the UK:
* Exposure Draft 21 issued by the Accounting Standards Committee September 1977 (ED 21).
* Exposure Draft 27 issued by the ASC October 1980.

The two exposure drafts issued in 1980 are the result of some close consultation between the FASB and the ASC, and are therefore in very close agreement. This is important. For although FAS 8 and ED 21 did not conflict on paper, due to the express permission given by ED 21 to the use of the temporal method required by FAS 8, their effect was that UK and US companies for the most part followed very different accounting principles in this field. The 1980 exposure drafts will make substantial changes in both countries, but the most radical changes will occur in US practice if the exposure draft becomes a fully fledged standard.

34

The accounting standards cover a variety of topics, but the topics which concern us in the context of current risk and its management, are:

1. The rates at which foreign currency transactions are recorded in the books of a single company.
2. The accounting treatment of forward contracts.
3. The rate at which assets and liabilities denominated in other currencies are 'translated' into the reporting currency of a single company in its annual balance sheet.
4. The treatment of currency gains and losses in a single company.

All the above topics concern the treatment of currency matters in the accounts of an individual company. They do not concern the consolidated accounts of a group of companies.

5. The rate at which the financial statements of foreign subsidiaries are translated into the parent reporting currency for the consolidated financial statements of a group of companies.
6. The treatment in the consolidated accounts of currency gains and losses resulting from such translation.

The accounting standard which has so far had the most startling impact on the approach to currency risk and its management, is FAS 8. It adopted the temporal method, and under it:

* assets and liabilities carried at current values are translated at the 'closing' rate, i.e. the spot exchange rate on the date of the balance sheet;
* assets and liabilities, revenues and expenses carried at historical costs are translated at historical rates of exchange, or at the rates ruling when the items were first recognized in the accounts;
* *all* currency gains and losses are reported as an undifferentiated part of operating profit or loss.

FAS 8 had two very great drawbacks. If a fixed asset was financed with a borrowing in the same currency, perhaps the local currency of the subsidiary holding the asset, that asset would be translated at the historical rate and the borrowing at the closing rate. The company had gone out of its way to avoid causing an imbalance in its net position in the currency, but FAS 8 had the effect of causing that very act of risk avoidance to show up currency gains or losses in the financial statements. The other great drawback was that it made all currency gains and losses part of the operating results. With heavily fluctuating spot rates this introduced great instability into operating results without necessarily shedding any objectively fair light on operating performance.

FAS 8, however, also had one great virtue. It recognized the importance of linking current values with current exchange rates, and historical values with historical exchange rates. Because there is a connection
between exchange rates and inflation, the topics of inflation accounting
and currency translation are closely linked, and FAS 8 came closer to
this ideal than the other standards and proposed standards that we are
examining.

FAS 8 is still in force at the end of 1980. As the new exposure draft of
August 1980 was approved by just a bare minority of the FASB, it is not
yet certain that it will become a standard and supersede FAS 8.

ED 21 never became a standard, but did in fact dominate accounting
practice in the United Kingdom during the last few years of the 1980s.
It permitted the temporal method, and therefore the essential rules of
FAS 8, but most companies in the United Kingdom adopted the alternative closing rate method. ED 21 did not draw a very clear distinction
between the treatment of currency gains or losses in one company on the
one hand and in consolidated accounts on the other. The most significant
rules for the closing rate method were:

* All assets and liabilities are translated at the closing rate, even if
  they are carried at historical values.
* *Realized* gains and losses from currency conversions are reported as
  part of the profit from ordinary operations.
* Translation gains or losses are not so reported. They are either
  shown as a separate item, after the profit after taxation, in the profit
  and loss account, or (if they relate to extraordinary items) as part of
  extraordinary items, or (if they relate to fixed assets and would not
  cause the appropriate reserve to become negative) as a movement
  in an appropriate reserve.
* Translation losses on borrowings denominated in a foreign currency
  (after deducting foreign currency cash or similar balances) may be
  matched against equal or smaller gains on translating the net book
  amount of overseas fixed assets: all that has to be equal here is the
  gain and the offsetting loss; they do not have to arise from the same
  foreign currency. This matching process is known as the 'cover'
  method.

ED 27, the proposed new standard for the United Kingdom, is a much
more detailed standard. It distinguishes between the rules applying in
any one company and those for consolidation, and it gives guidance on
the rate at which a foreign currency transaction should be recorded in
the books of account. Translation at closing rates is normally prescribed,
but in specific conditions the temporal method is mandatory. ED 27 does
not directly deal with forward contracts, whereas the 1980 exposure draft
of the FASB devotes two whole pages to that topic. This extract (para-

graphs 13, 18, 23–27) is reproduced in the Appendix at the end of this chapter.

Main provisions of ED 27

Recording foreign currency transactions in the books

This should be done by translating the transaction into the company's reporting currency at the date on which the transaction occurred using 'the exchange rate in operation on that date' or, where appropriate, 'the rate at which it is contracted to settle the transaction in the future'. Neither of these expressions is free from difficulty. We must assume that the former expression refers to the spot rate and the latter to either the forward rate at which the transaction has been covered forward (by means of a contract with a *bank* or other financial institution) or the rate at which it is agreed with the other party to the transaction itself (such as a supplier or customer) that the ultimate cash settlement price of the transaction is to be determined. (*Note*: forward cover is described in Chapter 9). A further difficulty is that it is not possible to speak unambiguously about *the* (spot or forward) rate in operation on a given day. Nor does the US draft overcome the difficulty by explaining that this is 'the' rate at which the transaction 'could be settled at the transaction date'. In one day there may well be thousands of such spot and forward rates, varying from minute to minute and from bank to bank. Many companies are no doubt using the *closing* rate quoted by some authoritative source like the *Financial Times*, which is itself an average of rates quoted by several banks at a particular time in the late afternoon of each dealing day.

Nor should this point be thought unimportant. For even if profits and net worth will not in the long run be affected by any uncertainty on this point, it is likely that the published *turnover* of a company will crystallize at the value at which each sale is initially recorded and translated, unless that figure happens to be provisional under the terms of the contract of sale.

Translation at an individual company's balance sheet date

This affects only monetary assets or liabilities. A non-monetary item like a fixed asset, once translated and recorded, will not need to be translated again. But a monetary item like a borrowing or a receivable, which is denominated in a currency other than the company's own reporting currency (the US draft refers to it as the 'functional' currency), needs to be retranslated at every reporting date at which it is outstanding. Unless the temporal method applies, this retranslation has to be done at the closing rate of exchange.

Treatment of gains and losses in an individual company

All currency gains and losses which arise in the accounts of an individual company must be treated as part of that company's ordinary profit or loss before taxation for the period. ED 27 sets out only one exception to this: where the event itself is disclosed as an extraordinary item, any currency gain or loss in respect of that item is also so disclosed. There is not, as there was under ED 21, an exception for fixed assets, and no separate line in the profit and loss account beneath the profit after taxation. (Appendix 5 to ED 27 does, however, invite submissions on whether the 'cover' method which applies *on consolidation* to net investments financed from currency loans, should be extended to currency loans owed by a holding company in its own accounts.)

The gain or loss which has to be treated as part of the profit or loss from ordinary operations is of course that part of an individual currency gain or loss which has occurred during the period. So if the risk existed throughout the period, the gain or loss arises from the difference between the opening and closing rate. If not, it may begin with the rate at which the transaction was initially recorded, or end with the rate at which it finally disappeared, or both, instead of the opening or closing rates.

In the case of trading risks, we must note that the early biography of the risk, from the rate used in the pricing decision up to the rate at which the transaction is recorded in the books, is not separately recorded or identified as a currency gain or loss at all. It will be an unidentified part of the trading margin, unless we calculate it by *ad hoc* analysis.

The implications of the rule that all gains and losses in the individual company must be treated as part of the ordinary pretax results, are far-reaching. Gains and losses from borrowings or from assets held in another currency, are part of the ordinary trading results, and so are those from currency borrowings of an intermediate holding company used to finance a net equity investment in a subsidiary in the same currency; unless of course the submissions invited in Appendix 5 of ED 27 cause the standard to be changed on this point. And any effect on the profit or loss in the separate accounts of a group company must remain intact in the consolidated results.

Group consolidation rules: the island or net investment theory

Both the FASB exposure draft of August 1980 and ED 27 take a big leap forward in the appreciation of the nature of balance sheet risk by considering and adopting the 'island' or net investment approach to translating the accounts of subsidiaries or associated companies for the purpose of the group consolidation.

ED 27 distinguishes between the case where a foreign subsidiary is in financial terms conducted as an extension of the parent company's own activity, and the case where the subsidiary has some measure of financial independence. In the former case the company might be financed from day to day through the parent company current account, in the latter from its own cash balance or local borrowings. In the former case, ED 27 regards the temporal method of translation, with rules close to those of FAS 8, as appropriate. In the latter case, which it regards as much more common, ED 27 takes the view that the parent company's interest in the subsidiary is really in the operation as a whole, and therefore in the net worth attributable to the parent, rather than in its separate assets and liabilities. Whereas in the former case each currency gain or loss of the subsidiary is effectively a cash gain or loss of the parent which should therefore recognize this in its accounts, the parent is only interested from year to year in the subsidiary's profit or loss and its changing net worth; its currency gains and losses should therefore also be seen in these terms. That is the criterion adopted by ED 27.

In Chapters 20 and 21 we shall review the implications of this net investment or 'island' approach. It faces us with the dilemma of whether a group is at risk on the individual assets and liabilities or on the whole of an operation conducted in a non-parent currency. The dilemma pervades the choice between managing accounting or transaction risk (are the short-dated receivables of such a subsidiary a short- or a long-maturity exposure?).

ED 27 squarely faces the main issue and declares that the net investment (defined as the capital and reserves plus long-term loans from the holding company) is the item on which the group is exposed to translation gains and losses. Consequently it would be wrong to translate individual assets and liabilities at different rates of exchange. Each such subsidiary is viewed as an integral island, not as a collection of assets and liabilities with different currency characteristics.

In Chapters 20 and 21 we shall see some difficulties in this concept, as indeed there are difficulties in any alternative concept that could be used instead. But the attention which the concept focuses on the relationship between a parent and a foreign subsidiary in this currency context must be welcomed as sheer gain.

Consolidation and 'cover' rules for the net investment approach

ED 27 lays down for all cases except the rare case where the temporal method is applicable:

* The net investment/closing rate method is mandatory both for subsidiaries and for associated companies dealt with by the equity method of accounting.
* The profit and loss account of a foreign subsidiary must be translated at the average rate for the period (ED 21 had permitted the alternative use of the closing rate).
* Assets and liabilities will be translated at the closing rate.
* Exchange gains and losses from (a) retranslating the opening net investment and (b) using the average rate, as distinct from the closing rate, for translating the profit and loss account, should be recorded as a movement on the reserves. It would not be appropriate to deal with such gains or losses in the profit and loss account because they do not represent or measure cash flow changes in the holding company. By contrast, all currency gains and losses in a single company actually or potentially affect its cash flows.
* Foreign branches of semi-independent status are treated as though they were subsidiaries: the net investment/closing rate method applies.
* Gains and losses on currency loans raised by a holding company to finance equity investments in foreign subsidiaries may be offset against losses or gains on retranslating the opening values of those equity investments, but only in the following circumstances:

    (a) the currency of the loan and of the equity investment must be the same;
    (b) the gain or loss on the debt can only be offset to the extent of the loss or gain on the equity investment;
    (c) the relationship between holding company and subsidiary must be one which justifies the use of the closing rate;
    (d) the offset treatment must be consistently applied year by year.

    The rules in ED 21 on this point were much more liberal. It should be remembered that this use of the 'cover' method is permitted only on consolidation, unless the submissions invited in Appendix 5 of ED 27 lead to its application to the separate accounts of a holding company's gains or losses on loans used to finance the net investment in a subsidiary.
* Where a subsidiary's local currency has depreciated against the parent currency and no reversal of that trend is in sight, so that the net investment in that company may be 'permanently impaired', that net investment should be covered by a provision.
* In countries with 'hyperinflation' it may be impossible to present the financial position of a local subsidiary without first revaluing its fixed assets at current values in the local financial statements before translating them at the closing rate.

An assessment of the 1980 US and UK exposure drafts

Ideal accounting conventions would harmonize the accounting and the true financial effects of currency risks and of hedging action to manage them. Where a company takes valid steps to neutralize true exposure, the ideal accounting rules would not create apparent gains or losses from the effects of those very steps. How successful ED 27 is in meeting this criterion, we cannot assess until we have fully explored the nature of balance sheet risk in Part 5 of this book. But the following example illustrates the problem:

Example 7   Single company buys foreign property

An American company buys real estate in Italy at a cost of Lit800 million. The spot rate is Lit800 = $1. The company could borrow either $1 million or Lit800 million to finance the purchase. The company's accounts are prepared under the rules of ED 27 which are the equivalent of those in the FASB's exposure draft issued August 1980. The following figures illustrate the effect (A) if it borrows dollars, (B) if it borrows lire, if alternatively

  (i) the property is sold for Lit800 million on the date of the next balance sheet *or* not sold, and
  (ii) the spot rate on that date is Lit720 *or* Lit880 = $1.

	(A) $ debt	(B) Lire debt
Spot rate Lit 720 = $1		
Dollar value of debt, $	1 000 000	1 111 111
Dollars realized from sale	1 111 111	1 111 111
Gain realized from sale	111 111	nil
Value of property in balance sheet if not sold	1 000 000	1 000 000
Net translation loss if not sold	nil	(111 111)
Spot rate Lit880 = $1		
Dollar value of debt	1 000 000	909 091
Dollars raised from sale	909 091	909 091
Loss realized from sale	(90 909)	nil
Value of property in balance sheet if not sold	1 000 000	1 000 000
Net translation gain if not sold	nil	90 909

So the company which wants to play safe under the 1980 exposure drafts, will borrow dollars, and the company which wants to protect itself against its true transaction risk, will borrow lire. It should be noted that the same result would emerge under FAS 8, but not under ED 21. It is also worth noting that if the US company had formed a local subsidiary to own the property and used the loan to acquire its equity, then the accounting result and transaction result would have been identical in the consolidated accounts under ED 27 and the FASB draft of August 1980.

Note: The book value in the example remains at $1 million under the rule in para 4 of ED 27 under which non-monetary assets, once translated and recorded in the reporting currency, require no subsequent translation.

Example 7 should simply be seen as an illustration of how accounting risk can conflict with true risk. When they do, the accounting conventions fall short of our ideal which avoids that conflict.

Judged by this criterion, ED 27 is an improvement on previous conventions, including FAS 8. But further improvements are needed, especially in connection with the cover method. Its use is much too restricted in ED 27. Thus it does not apply within one company, as we see in Example 7, and once this results in a gain or loss as part of ordinary income in the one company, that gain or loss has to go through into the group consolidation. Again ED 27 restricts the cover method to the net book value of the net worth of the subsidiary (plus long-term internal financing loans); the true exposure could be much larger. The cover method may apply only to borrowings raised by the *holding* company, whereas in many groups exchange controls or market conditions cause that borrowing to be made in a fellow subsidiary (where it will of course produce further 'gains or losses from ordinary trading' under ED 27). It could even be that ED 27 intends to restrict the cover method to the initial financing of a new subsidiary, and to deny it to a subsequent refinancing of that holding with a matching currency debt. These restrictions are serious in their implications.

Other shortcomings in ED 27 include its failure to deal with the possibility that large assets or liabilities may not be denominated in its local or functional currency; if our French subsidiary has a large dollar Eurobond, the group's French franc exposure is materially understated by the net investment as ED 27 defines it. Regrettable also is ED 27's failure to integrate inflation accounting with translation accounting except in cases of hyperinflation. The American August 1980 exposure draft does not even include the exception in the case of hyperinflation.

These shortcomings can cause conflicts between the objectives of managing accounting and true financial risk. The other great disappointment is that ED 27 (unlike the FASB exposure draft) fails to attend to the detailed problems of accounting for forward contracts. However, both exposure drafts give a satisfactory answer to the commonest and simplest question. Both specify that where a foreign currency transaction has been hedged by means of a forward contract, the accounting effect will effectively link the transaction with the hedge so as to make that hedge effective.

In stating this, the American draft unequivocally talks in terms of the *intention* with which the forward contract was entered into. If that concept could be widened in both standards so as to let the accounting effect of a currency *borrowing* be governed by the intention, much of the restrictiveness behind the new 'cover' rules could be relaxed.

This chapter has given a brief introduction to the accounting rules and the problems which affect currency risk and its management. A full discussion of the possible conflicts between the accounting conventions and the management of true financial risk must wait until Chapter 21, in other words, until we have examined the nature of true balance sheet risk in greater depth.

Appendix

Extracts from FASB Exposure Draft dated August 28 1980

Foreign Currency Translation

The following extracts are relevant to the treatment of forward exchange contracts

Foreign Currency Transactions

13. Foreign currency transactions produce foreign currency cash or foreign currency receivables and payables that are fixed in terms of the amount of foreign currency that will be received or paid. A change in exchange rates between the functional currency and the currency in which a transaction is denominated increases or decreases the amount of functional currency expected to be obtained upon settlement of foreign currency receivables or required to settle foreign currency payables. That increase or decrease in expected functional currency cash flows is an exchange gain or loss that generally shall be included in determining net income for the period in which exchange rates change. Likewise, exchange gains and losses (measured from the transaction date or the most recent intervening balance sheet date) realized upon settlement of foreign currency transactions generally shall be included in determining net income for the period in which the foreign currency transactions are settled. (The exceptions to the general requirements for inclusion in net income of exchange gains and losses from foreign currency transactions are set forth in paragraphs 18 and 24).

Investor-Investee Transactions and Transactions That Hedge Net Investments

18. Exchange gains and losses from translation of foreign currency transactions shall be included in determining net income (paragraph 13), except for the following exchange gains and losses which shall be reported as required by paragraph 33 and accumulated in the same separate component of stockholders' equity as are adjustments resulting from translation of foreign currency financial statements (paragraph 12):

a. Exchange gains and losses attributable to a foreign currency transaction that is intended to be, and is effective as, an economic hedge of a net investment in a foreign entity;
b. Exchange gains or losses attributable to foreign currency transactions between an investor and investee entity when that entity is consolidated, combined, or accounted for by the equity method in the investor's financial statments.

Forward Exchange Contracts

23. A forward exchange contract (forward contract) is an agreement to exchange different currencies at a specified future date and at a specified rate (the forward rate). A forward contract is a foreign currency transaction. A gain or loss on a forward contract that does not meet the conditions described in paragraphs 24 or 18 shall be included in determining net income in accordance with the requirements for other foreign currency transactions (paragraph 13).

24. A gain or loss on a forward contract that is intended to be a hedge of an identifiable foreign currency commitment (e.g., an agreement to purchase equipment) shall be deferred and included in the measurement of the basis of the related foreign currency transaction (e.g., the purchase of equipment in foreign currency). Losses on a forward contract shall not be deferred, however, if deferral could lead to recognizing losses in later periods. For example, a loss on a forward contract shall not be deferred if future revenue from the sale or other disposition of an asset is estimated to be less than the sum of (a) the asset's cost, including the deferred loss on the related forward contract, and (b) reasonably predictable costs of sale or disposal. A forward contract shall be considered a hedge of an identifiable foreign currency commitment provided all of the following conditions are met:

a. The forward contract is intended to be and at its inception is designated as a hedge of a foreign currency commitment.
b. The forward contract is denominated in the same currency as the foreign currency commitment, or a currency that is economically linked to that currency so as to move generally in tandem with it.
c. The foreign currency commitment is firm.

The portion of a forward contract that shall be accounted for pursuant to this paragraph is limited to the amount of the related commitment. If a forward contract that meets conditions (a) through (c) above exceeds the amount of the related commitment, the gain or loss pertaining to the portion of the forward contract in excess of the commitment shall be deferred to the extent that the forward contract is intended to provide a hedge on an after-tax basis. A gain or loss so deferred shall be included as an offset to the related tax effects in the period in which such tax effects are recognized; consequently, it shall not be included in the aggregate exchange gain or loss disclosure required by paragraph 31. A gain or loss pertaining to the portion of a forward contract in excess of the amount that provides a hedge on an after-tax basis shall not be deferred. Likewise, a gain or loss pertaining to a period after the transaction date of the related commitment shall not be deferred.

25. If a forward contract previously considered a hedge of a foreign currency commitment is sold or otherwise terminated before the transaction date, any deferred gain or loss shall continue to be deferred and accounted for in accordance with the requirements of paragraph 24.

26. A gain or loss (whether or not deferred) on a forward contract, except a forward contract of the type discussed in paragraph 27, shall be computed by multiplying the foreign currency amount of the forward contract by the difference between the spot rate at the balance sheet date and the spot rate at the date of inception of the forward contract (or the spot rate last used to measure a gain or loss on that contract for an earlier period). A transaction date (the date at which an unrecorded commitment becomes a recordable transaction) for a commitment that is hedged by a forward contract (paragraph 24) may occur during the period before the balance sheet date. In that case, the spot rate at the transaction date shall be used instead of the spot rate at the subsequent balance sheet date. The discount or premium on a forward contract (that is, the foreign currency amount of the contract multiplied

by the difference between the contracted forward rate and the spot rate at the date of inception of the contract) shall be accounted for separately from the gain or loss on the contract and shall be included in determining net income over the life of the forward contract. If a gain or loss is deferred under paragraph 24, however, the forward contract's discount or premium that relates to the commitment period may be included in the measure of the basis of the related foreign currency transaction when recorded.

27. A gain or loss on a forward contract that does not hedge an exposure (i.e., a speculation) shall be computed by multiplying the foreign currency amount of the forward contract by the difference between the forward rate available for the remaining maturity of the contract and the contracted forward rate (or the forward rate last used to measure a gain or loss on that contract for an earlier period). No separate accounting recognition is given to the discount or premium on such forward contracts that do not hedge an exposure.

PART 3

The Tools of Risk Management

CHAPTER 9

Currency Matching, Forward Cover, Financial Futures

This book does not set out to give a full technical description of the way the currency and international money markets operate. Others, especially Heywood (1978) and Donaldson (1980) have fully covered this topic.

We must, however, describe the principal risk management devices and their characteristics. There are broadly three classes of implements: those which avoid risk, those which hedge it, and those which reduce the task of management. Hedging is the partial or total elimination of a risk by some compensating action on the other side. The hedging tools for currency risk are forward cover, borrowing the exposed currency or creating extra assets in it, currency swaps, parallel loans, back-to-back loans and internal action like adjusting the timing of intragroup transactions. Tools which reduce the risk management task are the various forms of netting receipts and payments in the same currency; for this purpose currency accounts (also called 'hold' accounts) can be used so as to marry receipts and payments which are not due on the same day. The list is not exhaustive.

Avoidance of risk by matching

We have viewed currency risk as a currency mismatch either between selling price and cost or between assets and liabilities. The simplest way to pursue a defensive policy therefore is simply not to have the risk, by selling in the currency (or currencies) of cost and by financing all assets by debt in the same currency, leaving the parent company's capital and reserves invested in parent currency net assets. This rather simple method deserves more attention than it usually receives, so we shall list some of its main advantages at the beginning of Chapter 13.

It is worth mentioning that one of the tools, borrowing the currency in which we have surplus assets, can be used as both an avoidance and a hedging device. The difference is that it is an avoidance device when used to acquire the assets in the currency concerned, and a hedging device if used to hedge the exposure subsequently. We now turn to hedging devices.

Forward cover

A forward contract is a contract to exchange two currencies at an agreed future date at a predetermined rate of exchange. It is the future date which distinguishes it from a spot contract. An agreement to do the exchange today, for example, would be a spot contract.

Examples 8 and 9

We can best illustrate this from the *Financial Times* daily feature 'The dollar spot and forward' (from which we have eliminated three columns not relevant to the present purpose). For 'Italy' the entry might read as follows:

Last night Italy	Close	1 month	3 months
	836.50–837.00	7–8½ lire dis	18½–20 dis

This means that the 'average' bank towards the end of the previous night's trading might have offered to a corporate treasurer exchange contracts as follows:

	Rates available per one dollar		
	Spot	1 month forward	3 months forward
Bank buys lire for dollars	Lire	Lire	Lire
Spot rate	837	837	837
Forward discount	–	+ 8½	+20
Forward rate	837	845½	857
Bank buys dollars for lire			
Spot rate	836½	836½	836½
Forward discount	–	+ 7	+18½
Forward rate	836½	843½	855

Example 8

So if our costs are in dollars and our customer will pay us 837 000 lire in 3 months from yesterday, which yesterday evening would have fetched $1000 spot, we could sell those lire forward at Lit857 for $976.66, a discount of 2.334% (9.01% p.a.*) This $2^{1}/_{3}$% insurance premium would have protected us against a currency loss of unknown amount during the 3 months.

Example 9

But suppose our costs had been in lire and our invoice price fixed at $1,195.46. Last night this would have produced (at Lit836½) Lit1 000 000. The forward rate of Lit855 will produce a *certain* amount of Lit1 022 116 in 3 months, a *gain* of 2.2116%, or close to 9.14% p.a.† So this insurance 'premium' can have a *negative* cost, depending simply on which of the two currencies is being sold forward.

*$(0.97666)^4 = 0.90986$, a discount of 9.01422%
†$(1.022116)^4 = 1.09144$, a premium of 9.144%

Examples 8 and 9 illustrate some interesting points:

1. The rates quoted in the *Financial Times* represent those at which the bank would be willing to buy or sell the currency quoted:

	Sell lire	Buy lire	'Spread'
Spot	836½	837	½
1 month forward	843½	845½	2
3 months forward	855	857	2

The 'spread' is the bank's reward or margin, represented by the difference between its buy and sell rates. It is always wider for forward rates.

2. The forward discount must be added to the spot rate because the lira is at a forward discount to the dollar, so that we get more lire per dollar in the forward market. If we had quoted the rate as dollars per lire, the forward discount would need to be deducted from the spot rate to compute the forward rate.

3. The same feature in the *Financial Times* quoted the interest rate for three months Eurodollars at a middle rate of 9½% per annum and that for Eurolire at 19¼%. The difference of 9¾% is not far from the 9.1% forward discount per annum produced by the forward rates for 3 months. This is not a coincidence. Forward rates are largely governed by the spot rate plus or minus the difference between the Eurocurrency interest rates – the bank does not normally run a book on its forward deals. If it has sold us 3 months lire forward against dollars at Lit855, it will go into the market and borrow dollars for 3 months at 9½% p.a. and lend lire at 19¼% for 3 months. At the end of the 3 months it can repay the dollars to the market from the dollars which we must then deliver to the bank, and it can pay us the greater amount of lire from the combined total of (a) the lire it collects back from the market, plus (b) the extra interest it has earned on the difference between the two interest rates. The bank has completely hedged its forward deal with us in this manner, and neither we nor the bank have taken any chance on the currency movement in the 3 month period. Our forward contracts and their borrowing and lending contracts with the market were all for amounts determined on day 1 of the period.

Forward contracts do not solve all problems

At first sight therefore, forward contracts look like a panacea for all currency risk problems. They do, however, have some limitations:

* The banks can only deal forward to the extent that they can freely borrow and lend a currency interbank. This cuts out some currencies like the Indian rupee, the Nigerian naira or the Brazilian cruzeiro for which there is no such free interbank market.

   * For the same reason, even where there is such a market, if the
market for a currency is limited in the size or maturities of transactions which it can handle at fixed rates of interest, then the forward market will be restricted in the same way. Consequently it is
only for very few currencies that forward contracts are possible for
as long ahead as 5 years, and many markets are limited to 12
months or less.

   * Forward contracts are strictly binding and must be complied with.

In Example 8 we undertook to the bank to deliver 837 000 lire in 3
months in exchange for $976.66. We have to find those 837 000 lire even
if our customer is late and does not deliver the 837 000 lire to us by that
time. Of course this need not be a problem to us because we can either
roll the contract over (see Example 16 in Chapter 15) or we can borrow
the 837 000 lire for a few days, if we are not constrained by exchange
controls, and repay when we receive them from our customer. Similarly,
if our customer pays them too soon, we can keep them on a lire bank
account until we need them to close out our forward contract. But this
would be a severe problem if the receipt from the customer were not
merely early or late, but never came at all. This could happen if we had
covered forward a mere tender, and then failed to be successful in ob-
taining the contract. In that case we must buy the lire spot at a rate we
could not predict when we entered into the forward contract, and might
incur a greater loss than we tried to hedge when we first took out the
forward contract. We come back to this difficulty in Chapters 12 and 15.

Example 16 in Chapter 15 shows that if we roll over or extend a
forward contract, we strictly close it out and enter into a new contract
for the extension period. The operation involves an immediate cash receipt or payment and either a further premium or a discount, depending
on which currency is at a forward premium to the other. The overall
profit effect is seldom dramatic.

The complications of rolling forward or borrowing lire for the period
of delay, or keeping them on a lire bank account if they arrived early,
could have been avoided if we had taken out a forward option contract.
The option here is not *whether* we wish to deliver the lire to the bank,
but *when* within a specified period called the option period, for example,
on any date in the month of June. The only snag with that arrangement
is that the bank will give us the forward rate for the worst date in the
option period from our point of view. In the present case we should be
paying the bank a discount on selling lire, and the highest discount
would have been that for 30 June, and that is the date for which we
should have been given the forward rate. Had we been buying lire
forward against dollars, the forward rate would have been the rate for
1 June, again the worst rate for us. This is the cost of taking out a
forward option period, which has to be weighed against the administra-

tive saving on the alternative of rolling the contract over for a few days, for example.

Finally, although we must not take out forward contracts for an exposure which we may not have (like the tender we mentioned above), we can of course use forward contracts for an exposure which does not involve the delivery or payment of the currency concerned. One example is where we sell in our own currency of US dollars to a customer in Belgium, but at a price so fixed that all deviations from a stated rate of Belgian francs per dollar are for our account. Our effective exposure is as if we were selling in Belgian francs. If we then sell the Belgian francs forward, we have to buy the Belgian francs in at the spot rate on the date of payment, so as to close out our forward contract at a gain or loss which should just cancel out the loss or gain we make on the currency adjustment formula in the agreed price. We could do exactly that if the exposure was not ours, but that of our Belgian subsidiary, and that subsidiary could not for some reason cover it forward under Belgian conditions. Our gain or loss in the United States would then balance out the loss or gain made by the Belgian company.

Forward cover, then, is an excellent hedging device, provided we have a definite risk to hedge, and subject to some limitations mentioned above.

Currency futures trading

Trading in financial futures is a relatively new weapon in the currency field. But in the Chicago International Money Market it has become very big business. Other markets are opening, and one is expected to open in London in 1982

Futures trading needs to be done in standard units or modules. On the Chicago I.M.M. we get units of £25,000 and DM 125,000 for example. There are only four quarterly maturity dates each year, and the longest maturity is 18 months. There are costs and complex rules for margin deposits to be taken into account.

Banks derive valuable opportunities for arbitrage in this market, and the linkage between futures trading and the bank forward markets should in the long run be a benefit to the task of currency management.

It is possible however that companies with ready access to well developed bank forward markets will find these cheaper, more flexible and better tailored to their precise hedging requirements. Companies may well find interest rate futures more attractive than currency futures.

References

Donaldson, J. A. (1980). *Corporate Currency Risk*, The Financial Times Business Information Ltd., London.
Heywood, J. (1978). *Foreign Exchange and the Corporate Treasurer*, Black, London.

CHAPTER 10

Borrowings, Back-to-Back Loans, Swaps, Currency Deposits

Currency borrowings

Along with forward cover, currency borrowings are the major currency risk management device. In many ways they are the most flexible device in a treasurer's armoury. They can be used against new or old risks, against balance sheet and also trading exposures.

Currency borrowings are of course closely related to forward contracts. If we are due to receive dollars from a customer in 12 months, and our costs are in sterling, let us assume that the interest cost of 12 months sterling is 5% higher than that of 12 months Eurodollars. In that case we could normally expect to sell the dollars forward for 12 months at a 5% gain against today's spot rate. Alternatively, we could borrow Eurodollars for 12 months, to be repaid out of the receipt from the customer at the end of the 12 months, and this would give us an interest saving of 5%. Subject to any tax or accounting complications, we should be indifferent between the two courses of action. And little wonder. For what we have done by borrowing instead of covering forward, is what the bank would have done to cover its own position after buying our dollars forward from us instead.

In practice we may well not be indifferent. Quite apart from any different tax and accounting effects, we might be in surplus cash with no need for borrowings; in that case our saving would be the gap between the rates of interest we can earn on sterling deposits and the Eurodollar rate. Again, if we did have sterling debt, this might be at variable overdraft rates, and not at a fixed rate for the 12 months, and we might have reason to expect that the average cost of overdrafts over the period will fall short of the fixed rate for 12 months. In any case, the forward premium is calculated from the Eurosterling rate, which is likely to differ from our domestic sterling cost of funds. But all these reservations leave intact the fundamental point that forward cover and currency borrowing are closely related and financially not very different operations.

Currency borrowings can be more flexible as an exposure management device than forward cover; for if market conditions permit, we can borrow for flexible periods, that is, with easy prepayment or rollover conditions, and if we desire, with variable rather than fixed rates of interest. And the limitations on the length of period for which forward cover is available, are often limitations on *fixed* interest funds. Variable interest rate funds may well be available for much longer periods (this is discussed in Chapter 22). Obviously, where a currency is not freely traded, a thin market or exchange control regulations may well make that currency unavailable both for forward contracts and for borrowings. The restrictions which this places on both devices are likely to be similar.

Borrowings, however, are more difficult for a company which is close to its borrowing limits because it is already heavily geared; and as we have seen, they are likely to be unattractive to a company so liquid that it does not need to borrow for financial reasons. However, where borrowings are practicable, they are an answer to the risk caused by an excess of assets over liabilities in the currency concerned.

In Example 10 we see an American company, Columbia, which has an excess of sterling assets over sterling debt in its consolidated balance sheet. By borrowing an extra £10 million = $20 million, it can remedy this, provided it immediately converts the newly borrowed sterling into dollars and repays dollar debts. If it kept the £10 million sterling as a sterling asset (for example, investing in sterling securities), the mismatch would remain undiminished.

Example 10   Columbia (consolidated balance sheet) $ millions before and after £10 million sterling drawdown

	Before	After
Dollar net operating assets	150	150
Sterling net operating assets	50	50
	200	200
Share capital and reserves	130	130
Dollars owed to banks	40	20
Existing sterling debt (£15 million)	30	30
New sterling borrowing (£10 million)	–	20
	200	200
Net sterling assets	20	nil

Example 10 clearly shows that after drawdown the total sterling debt is now $50 million, which covers the sterling net operating assets. The sterling exposure is now fully hedged, subject to any tax or accounting effects.

Borrowing against an income stream in a foreign currency

We have established that we can with equal effect use a borrowing instead of forward cover for a receipt due in 12 months. But it is sometimes claimed that a company can safely borrow another currency and take advantage of the lower interest rates prevailing in that currency, as long as the company 'has income' in that currency. Does this hold good if the debt is not from the outset designed to be repaid from precisely identified future receipts?

In Chapter 4 we defined trading currency risk as the risk to the profit margin on a commercial sale in a currency which is not the currency of cost, from an adverse movement in the exchange rate from that rate which had been used in the original pricing decision:

Example 11

A company in the United Kingdom borrows Swiss francs 3 900 000 for a year at a time when the spot rate is Swiss Fr3.9 = £1, 12 months sterling costs 15½% and 12 months Swiss francs 5½%. The forward rate for 6 months is Swiss Fr3.705 = £1. We have no Swiss franc assets at present, but we shall have a Swiss franc income stream because we are starting to sell office machines, for which our desired sterling price is £1000 each, to Switzerland. Payment is due to us after 180 days. Our first consignment we price at Swiss Fr3705 per machine, as our UK competitors are sure to use the forward rate in their pricing. In sterling we shall at Swiss Fr3.9 receive an effective price of £950 if we use the Swiss Fr3705 received for each machine as a part repayment of the loan. We receive cash for each machine after 180 days. By borrowing at 5½% instead of 15½% we have therefore saved £1000 at 10% for 6 months = £50. Together with the £950 sterling receipt we have therefore achieved a total benefit of £1000 which was our desired sterling price. The hedge worked because we fixed our price with the interest rate and spot and forward rate structure in mind.

Now 4 months later sterling has fallen by 10% to Swiss Fr3.51 = £1. Interest rates are now 6% for Swiss francs and 11% for sterling, an annual differential of 5%, and the 6 months forward rate is Swiss Fr3.4223 = £1. We go on treating each sale as repaying part of the loan at Swiss Fr3.9 = £1, but by now the competition is forcing us to reduce our price to Swiss Fr3422.30. Our effective sterling receipt at Swiss Fr3.9 is then £877.51, and the interest saved on the *desired* price of £1000 at 5½% per annum (11%–5½%) is £27.50, making our total effective receipt £905.01, or £94.99 less than intended.

Like all examples of this kind, it shows a loss where there might on other assumptions have been a gain. But it illustrates that the borrowing of Swiss francs against the mere existence of an income stream in that currency may be a very smart deal or a disaster, but what it certainly is not is a hedge of the trading risk. It would only hedge the trading risk if all pricing decisions could use the spot rate at which we sold the borrowed francs, and the original forward exchange and interest rates. If, as we assumed here, the market forces us to reduce our Swiss franc prices, the hedge ceases to protect us. In the example we also assumed that each sales receipt will be used to repay part of the loan. If we do not do this, then we are even more remote from the concept of hedging the trading exposure.

It is important to remember that the loan would be a perfectly good hedge against an assumed Swiss Fr3.9 million level of *receivables*, if we could regard such a rolling level as reliable. But that assumption presupposes that we do not bother to hedge the underlying trading risk at all up to the point at which we have receivables on the balance sheet. Each sale and its specific pricing decision is ignored until there is a receivable on the balance sheet, so that there is no hedge against whatever movements may occur in the exchange rate between the pricing decision and the appearance of the receivable on the balance sheet or exposure matrix. *After that* any further movements are hedged by the loan. But by that time we could be locking ourselves into a loss by that hedge. Even that could be a better policy than exposing the company to a further deterioration in the exchange rate, but it does not amount to a safe policy. What we are hedging is the balance sheet risk which results from an unmanaged trading risk, not the original trading risk.

Currency borrowings raise other complications which are discussed in Chapter 25.

Back-to-back loans, parallel loans, currency swaps and two-way hedges

The first three of these were not primarily designed to deal with currency risks, but rather with financing problems and exchange controls. All of them differ from currency borrowings and the other risk management tools we have discussed, because they are essentially between two commercial parties, not between a commercial party and a financial institution. Technically one of these deals may be so arranged that a bank intermediates between two commercial parties. This is sometimes done to deal with the credit risk. But in such cases the deal will still not come about until two commercial parties are found who have an equal and opposite interest in concluding the deal.

Example 12

English Industries Ltd agrees with Wallaby Industries Ltd of Sydney, New South Wales, that English will lend Wallaby £5 million and Wallaby will lend English Aust. $10 million for 7 years. This is a *back-to-back loan*. Alternatively each of them agrees to make the loan to the other's subsidiary in his own (the lender's) country. That is a *parallel loan*. Thirdly the agreement could be that English will pay to Wallaby £5 million and Wallaby Aust $10 million to English now, and that each has an option at some future date to require both payments to be reversed at that same rate of exchange of Aust. $2 = £1. That would be a *currency swap*. A swap differs from a forward contract because there is an initial mutual cash payment. In this case there is the further element that the subsequent reversal of the transaction is merely an option, not a definite commitment. Finally the two parties may agree to make no initial cash exchange, but merely to exchange currencies at maturity at the prearranged exchange rate. This is a bilateral forward contract and differs from other forward contracts because it is between two commercial parties for an unusually long period.

All such deals involve considerable tax and credit problems, as well as sometimes exchange control rules. Rights of set-off and top-up clauses sometimes protect the credit exposure. To compensate for the difference in interest rates in the two countries interest or a net annual amount for the difference is often charged, and a swap may attract a fee in lieu of that differential.

All these matters are highly complex, but the greatest difficulty usually is to find two commercial parties with an equal and opposite interest in such a deal. Small wonder then that such transactions are rare in practice and seldom for more than 5 to 7-year maturities; well short of the life-span of many balance sheet risks.

However, the examples which are found in real life show that most of them come about to overcome the problems of exchange controls in one or other of the countries. There are very few examples where a currency hedge was the main motive. Back-to-back and swap deals enable one party to invest outside its own country and the other to finance its local subsidiary without remitting fresh convertible funds into the exchange control net.

And yet these deals can in principle be used to hedge currency risks. The effect is identical with that of a currency borrowing. But there are usually easier ways of dealing with the risks. Back-to-back and swap deals should be borne in mind however, when exchange controls become an obstacle to the normal hedging devices. Mutual forward contracts are a theoretical option, but tend to run into even greater tax problems than the other alternatives.

Hedging an excess of liabilities

We have so far dealt mainly with the need to hedge excess assets rather than excess liabilities, and for this reason we have looked at currency borrowings which are an answer to an excess assets position in a given currency. In practice, however, we often find that companies' actual problems arise from excess liabilities in a currency.

In the field of trading risk we also get the case where we have costs, but no sales, in a currency, usually if a supplier happens to be selling to us in a currency in which we are not selling. In this latter case, the forward purchase of his currency at the time that we place our orders is often the best hedge.

But if we have excess liabilities, the best answer may well be the creation of extra assets, like bank deposits in the same currency. We could look upon this as negative borrowing. The same device is often used to hedge a purchase if forward cover is either not suitable or not available. Instead of waiting until the date we have to pay, we buy the supplier's currency instantly the day we order, and place it on deposit until we need the currency to make our payment.

Whenever we create deposits in the currency in which we had surplus liabilities, we must of course take care to match the maturities so that we have the deposits available to finance the repayment of the liabilities when they fall due.

One problem with the creation of such deposits is that we could be causing an overlap of financial assets and liabilities, and thus artificially increase the gearing of the group balance sheet. If we have equity of $10 million and debt of $8 million, our debt: equity gearing ratio is 80%. If we now borrow another $2 million in order to deposit $2 millions worth of Swiss francs, the total assets financed will rise to $20 million from the previous $18 million, and our total debt will now be $10 million, or 100% of the equity. And 100% could be in breach of a loan covenant or just too high a gearing for both our financial health and our share price.

This gearing problem could be overcome if we could arrange to deposit the Swiss francs with one of our *existing* lenders, with a formal right of set-off built into the terms. This would leave the gearing unchanged, except to the (usually minor) extent that subsequent currency movements make the value of the deposit exceed the currency equivalent of the borrowings covered by the right of set-off. But the greater difficulty may be to find a lender with whom we can deposit the Swiss francs and obtain the set-off rights. This is particularly the case where the existing debt is owed to public debenture or loan stock holders, and not to banks.

Hedges can cost money, and in this case the cost is likely to be that it will cost us a much higher interest rate to borrow the funds which we convert into Swiss francs, than we can earn on the Swiss franc deposit. But presumably this interest loss is less painful than the penalty for prematurely repaying the Swiss franc debt which we wish to hedge. Otherwise, we should of course prepay.

CHAPTER 11

Netting of Exposures, Hold Accounts, The Exposure Matrix, Leading and Lagging

Netting is a most widely used technique in currency risk management. A company which finds itself with receivables and payables in some foreign currency, takes the *net* amount, thinks of this as the exposure, and decides either to hedge it or to leave it unhedged.

In the field of balance sheet risks we have already assumed that this is the way to look at them. If we have several subsidiaries in France, with French franc assets and liabilities, then it is clearly the combined *net* total which constitutes our exposure, that is, we deduct the liabilities from the assets in the process of calculating it.

Obviously in the trading case, if today we contract to sell a consignment of goods for $1000, payable 180 days from now, and we simultaneously place an order for components needed to execute that order for $600, also payable 180 days from now, then we as a sterling-based company, with all our other costs in sterling, have a net exposure of only $400 on that order. If we sold $400 forward, we should be left with no unhedged risk, and our action would meet the requirements of the most defensive policy. If, however, we had an aggressive policy, and took the view that in the period of 6 months the dollar will be rising against sterling, we could either leave the position unhedged, expecting to make a gain on the net $400, or we could get even more aggressive and buy the $600 forward and leave the $1000 receipt unhedged. In that case we expect to make a gain on $1000, less of course the forward premium (if any) on the $600.

We have so far assumed that our receipts and payments in the netted currency are exactly synchronized, that is, are due on the same day. If they are not, then we can use a dollar bank account ('hold' account), which we can keep either in credit or overdrawn, according to whether our receipt or our payment occurs first. Clearly, such hold accounts substantially widen the scope for netting. For if we had to convert either the receipt or the payment into our home currency, for any reason, *before* the other side of the netting transaction was ready for its spot exchange conversion, the risk would not be avoided and the netting process would be ineffective.

Companies with a multitude of currency exposures take this concept a step further, and arrange for their corporate treasurer to receive a daily, weekly or monthly worldwide matrix which shows all receivables and payables due or expected in each of the next 3, 6 or more months (or weeks or days), leaving him to manage the net exposure by hedging 100% or 75% or 50% or 25% or none of that exposure, depending on the view he takes of the likely movement in that currency against the home currency, and in particular whether he considers that the spot rate on each maturity will be more or less favourable than the forward rate at which he could deal now. This is a widely practised method, so widely that many of the currency forecasting services on offer to corporate treasurers express their advice in these terms, for example, 'cover payables' or 'cover receivables 75%'.

This exposure matrix system assumes that receivables and payables *maturing* simultaneously constitute a nettable risk. In other words, the underlying principle concerns itself rather less with the birth of each risk than with its death. The validity of this approach will be tested in Example 15 in Chapter 14. It is clear however, that the concept of netting must result in a significant saving in currency dealing costs.

Leading and lagging

This is the practice of lengthening or shortening the terms of intercompany trade credit, usually within an international group of companies.

Suppose, for instance, we are a French company with a subsidiary in Italy to which we regularly sell a stream of goods, giving the Italian company 90 days to pay. If the treasurer expects a fall in the lira against the French franc, he may decide to require the Italian company to pay cash against documents on the day of delivery, in other words, reduce the trade credit from 90 days to zero. In aggressive currency management terms this is clearly successful. If the lira duly falls against the franc, the group will realize a gain. Conversely it will realize a loss if the treasurer was wrong and the lira rises against the franc. Both comparisons are with the alternative of continuing the period of 90 days credit. On the other hand, whether leading and lagging amounts to defensive currency risk management, that is, whether it constitutes an act of hedging, depends on whether in our example it brings the French group's net lira assets closer to nil or not. Leading and lagging is best seen as a manipulation of the balance sheet exposure. Suppose the treasurer's reduction of the credit period reduces net lira assets in the group by (say) the equivalent of Fr90 000. This would completely eliminate the exposure if the original net lira position was Fr90 000. If it was more than a positive Fr90 000, the action taken would still have served to reduce the exposure. If the original net lira position had been negative (more lira liabilities than assets), the treasurer would actually have aggravated the group exposure by withdrawing trade credit.

To sum up, then, leading and lagging is useful as an aggressive risk management device. If we wish to use it as a hedging or defensive device, we must analyse its effect on the net total position of the whole group, and ascertain whether the change in intercompany credit terms will bring the existing exposure closer to nil.

PART 4

Managing Trading Risks and Intragroup Risks

CHAPTER 12

Life-cycle of a Currency Exposure: from Conception to Death

In Chapter 4 we defined *trading* currency risk as the risk of an adverse movement in the exchange rate between the rate *assumed when we commit ourselves to a price* in one currency against a cost in another, for example when we submit a tender for a contract or issue a price list. In such cases the currency risk exists as a potentiality before it is actual, that is, before we have won our contract or booked any sales under the price list which we have issued.

Such a trading exposure progressively comes to an end when we collect the price or prices of the goods sold, or (if we sell in our own currency but buy in another currency) when we pay for our purchases in the unmatched currency. A number of things can happen between beginning and end. It is convenient to describe the stages as follows:

Conception   : when we commit ourselves to the mismatch.
Birth   : when the commitment becomes a commercial or contractual reality: it has ceased to be unilateral.
Anniversaries: any annual reporting dates at which interim gains or losses may be ascertained.
Death   : the end of the exposure when we are free to convert the receipt or payment into the other currency and thus measure the final cash gain or loss.

The antenatal period

It is convenient to speak about the period between conception and birth as the antenatal period. It is the period during which we have committed ourselves to a risk which will come into actual existence if a trading partner, that is, a customer or a supplier, accepts our offer and holds us to the commitment. This antenatal risk is by no means a feature of all trading where there is a mismatch. For example if we are a sterling company with sterling costs and sell from stock at prices quoted at the time of sale in dollars, then conception and birth coincide and there is no antenatal period.

The existence of this antenatal period is one of the most important and sometimes neglected features of the theory of currency risk management. The main reason for this is that it is generally not advisable to take hedging action during the antenatal period. Why is it not advisable? Because the hedge itself, that is, the forward contract or currency borrowing, needs to be closed out or repaid *at a spot rate which cannot be predicted*, if the risk which we are hedging never comes into being, for example if we fail to win our tender. The worst example of this is undoubtedly the very large tender, illustrated in Example 17 in Chapter 15.

It is sometimes objected that the big tender example is extreme and exceptional, and that in real life there is often a great volume of antenatal risks, forming part of steady and large volumes of sales, which can be predicted. There will always be a rock-bottom volume of sales which is not yet booked but which obviously will be booked, and which can therefore safely be hedged without risking the closing-out trauma which we have just described. This is true in a very important sense, and is one reason why we define the antenatal period as ending at the point where we can be *commercially* certain of a sale. But it is vital to remember here that the conception of a risk *begins* with the *pricing decision*. It is no good thinking we have hedged a trading risk as a trading risk if we are not controlling the currency outcome of the risk in relation to the exchange rate used in the pricing decision. Chapter 14, in particular, goes into this point intensively. But if we accept that there are some predictable sales which will flow from the pricing decision we have in mind, but have not yet been booked, and that therefore we can legitimately cover those predictable sales forward, we are still left with a considerable field of antenatal risk. And this considerable field is one of the most difficult areas of risk management. The only complete defence is to sell in the currency of cost; perhaps we should call that contraception. We must remember too that antenatal risk can theoretically come on the purchasing side. In a really tough case we may be in the very undesirable position where we have had to tender before we had a major supplier committed to an acceptable price. If so, we could effectively be committed at both ends (for if the customer buys, we *must* purchase from this supplier or another) and our combined antenatal period will not be over until both the purchase and the sale, whichever comes later, are agreed.

Balance sheet risks

So far in this chapter we have only dealt with trading risk. In principle the sequence of conception–birth–anniversaries–death applies equally to balance sheet risks. What is less clear is whether in practice we actually encounter the antenatal problem in this field.

We defined balance sheet risk in Chapter 5 as a mismatch between assets and liabilities in any one currency other than the reporting currency. In Chapter 6 we ran into some difficulties about the concept of balance sheet risks as transaction risks, but decided that the concept was valuable, as it was desirable to manage balance sheet risks for periods which look beyond the next annual reporting date.

There are really three important differences between actual instances of balance sheet and trading risks. One is that balance sheet risks have to be looked at in total. This is not to say that if we are about to buy a manufacturing company in another country, we must not look at this as a new and separate currency risk, which we must finance as a one-off problem. But this is not sufficient description of the task of balance sheet risk management. The task also involves a constant review, at least once a year and probably more frequently, of the entire balance sheet position of the group. For practically no asset or liability configuration is likely to be static. Current assets fluctuate up and down, their currency composition may vary from time to time, fixed assets are a changing population against which we also provide depreciation. Borrowings and payables fluctuate in any dynamic business. If we buy a new subsidiary, we have certainly added an order of magnitude of assets in a given currency which we must assume will stay at approximately that level, but it certainly will not stay at *exactly* that level as long as it trades. So every major addition to assets or liabilities needs a specific effort at currency management, but the balance sheet risk also needs regular overall review and management. That is the first of the three differences.

The second is that it is in fact hard to find antenatal problems in balance sheet risks. If we tender for a contract from a sterling base in a currency other than sterling, we have little choice. We are stuck with an antenatal exposure. But if, for example, we decide to buy a large foreign currency asset for a price in its currency, we normally have the choice of financing the purchase in that same currency, and we do not normally have to commit ourselves to the purchase before we have settled the method of financing.

The third difference between trading and balance sheet risks is the difficulty of defining a maturity date for them. It is of course true that monetary assets and liabilities tend to have known maturities, but most non-monetary items have no definite lives, so that for example a policy of avoiding balance sheet risks by matching assets with liabilities of identical maturity, is more easily declared desirable than implemented. We have already spotted this problem in Chapter 6, and shall deal with it in Chapter 23.

We can therefore sum up this examination of the life-cycle of a currency risk in two statements. First, the life-cycle can consist of concep-

68

tion, birth, anniversaries and death, but antenatal risks are a feature of some important trading risks only. Secondly, the total life-span of trading exposures is in general more predetermined or predictable than that of balance sheet exposures, some of which die at unknown future dates, and are in this respect more analogous to human beings.

CHAPTER 13

Managing Ordinary Trading Risks: Some Methods

Our definition of trading currency risk in Chapter 4 had as its critical feature the threat of achieving a worse cash receipt in the currency of cost than was assumed in the pricing decision. This would occur if the actual currency conversion turned out less favourable than was assumed in that decision. This central feature of comparing the outturn with the exchange rate used in the pricing decision will run right through our discussion of trading risk in the next four chapters.

Avoidance by matching

The policy which avoids this risk simply and cheaply is to sell in the currency of cost. It avoids all risk, antenatal and postnatal, and requires no staff specialized in currency matters. It might, however, lose some business with some customers.

Avoidance by matching also involves two minor technical problems.

First, if we have costs in several currencies, we should sell in the currency with the largest costs and hedge the purchase costs in the other currencies. Secondly we noted in Chapter 4 that where this means selling in a currency which is not the reporting currency of the selling subsidiary or of the parent company, we leave the profit exposed or to be managed as a balance sheet risk.

Example 13

The German subsidiary of a US parent manufactures with D-mark costs and sells in D-marks, making a net margin of 15%. If we believe that at worst the D-mark can fall by 12% against the dollar before the profit can be distributed to the United States as a dividend (and ignoring German tax), then the worst loss from this exposure is 12% of 15% = 1.8%. If the subsidiary had not invoiced its sales in D-marks, it would have taken a currency risk on the whole 100% instead of just 15% of the price.

This policy of avoiding risk by matching currency of price and cost receives relatively little attention or respect in the literature. And yet it must be a serious option. It is surely better than any unprofessional attempt to beat the market, or even uncritical neglect. In a business environment which becomes ever more complex, its simplicity alone should commend it.

Accepting selected risks and covering forward at birth

Nevertheless, a company with at least some professional risk management resources will not always find that this risk-free policy is the best. This is because there are customers from whom we can get a better price fixed in their currency but sold forward into ours, than in our own currency, in which we incur our costs. So whenever our marketing intelligence tells us that a hedged exposure gives us a better price than a price in the currency of cost, the hedged exposure is the better policy. But we must qualify this by insisting that it must be an iron rule to cover forward at birth, and that the policy does not apply where we have a significant antenatal risk. Antenatal risk, it will be recalled, arises whenever we have to commit ourselves to a quoted price in an unmatched currency some time before the customer has to enter into a contract to buy from us. For during that interval the currency can move against us, and as we saw in Chapter 12, we cannot safely cover the risk forward before we have a sale.

The same principle is true of purchases: we can often buy more advantageously by buying in the supplier's currency and covering our payment forward.

Accepting selected unhedged risks

In some situations companies reasonably decide to sell in unmatched currencies without hedging, as a matter of calculated risk. A classic case is where there are good and continuing reasons to believe those currencies to be stronger than the currency of cost. Many Italian manufacturers have a policy of selling to Germany in D-marks. After all, the D-mark is normally on a rising trend against the lira. The exceptions are few and modest. Of course, if the company has the risk management resources available, it will sometimes judge it better to collect the often generous forward premium. But a policy of staying unhedged will normally be safe and profitable. Yet that same Italian company should know better than to sell to (say) Brazil in cruzeiros. But policies like these still need to be made consciously and professionally, and reviewed at least once a year. Currencies can change their characteristics, as did sterling on attaining oil-producing status, and the French franc since de Gaulle.

We have so far dealt with three predetermined and consistent policies:

1. Sell only in the currency of cost: avoid risk by matching.
2. Accept selected risks and automatically hedge them.
3. Accept open risks in selected 'strong' currencies of sale.

These three policies are cheap to implement. The second is a little more costly because it involves some forward dealing and therefore some skilled staff. But none of them require an exposure management overhead with staff and information resources needed for that purpose.

Fourth method: 'to hedge or not to hedge'

There is, however, a fourth method which does need those resources, and which receives more attention in the literature than the other three methods together. We might call this the 'to hedge or not to hedge' method, although many might more readily recognize it as the exposure matrix method. This method periodically, say once a month, reviews all exposures, especially those which arise from buying and selling. Each periodical review assesses whether they should be covered forward or not. The criterion is whether the forward rate looks more favourable than either the expected spot rate on maturity or perhaps a future forward rate for that same maturity. Each review crystallizes the decision whether to deal at the then available forward rate.

Method four takes many forms, which depend on the trading and organizational characteristics of the company or group. Companies give different periods of credit, sell in different numbers of currencies, have different typical sizes of transaction, different numbers and frequencies of sale. They also have different group structures, reporting systems, and above all different corporate attitudes to currency risk. An important point here is what level of risk is regarded as catastrophic, and how many of the group's transactions are above that catastrophe threshold. And in a decentralized group the individual profit centres might each consider their catastrophe level to be lower than the group centre sees it. If that happens, an intolerable conflict could arise between the group treasurer and the individual profit centres.

A general discussion of organizational problems caused by currency risk is contained in Part 7 of this book.

Complete centralization for method four

That kind of conflict can only be resolved by centralizing currency risks to the point where all receivables and payables are transferred to the corporate centre at predetermined home currency values. The corporate treasurer then has to manage the currency risks as a self-contained profit centre in its own right. This can take the form of a separate finance company, which 'buys' the receivables from the operating units and accepts from them the transfer of their payables at the agreed exchange rates. Whether the finance company makes a profit or a loss on these risks then becomes a measure of its success in managing those risks.

The expense of such complete centralization should not be underestimated. Even if the treasurer does not operate a separate finance company with its company law overhead, annual accounts, audit etc., the task of taking over all trade balances must involve a considerable expense in expert staff and a fresh set of management interfaces. There will be disagreements about the intercompany transfer values ('Why can I not get the benefit of forward premiums? My competitors get it!'). And there will of course be the expensive array of online video terminals for spot and forward rates, data of exposures from the operating units, interfaces with brokers and bankers and a battery of telephone and telex lines by way of logistic support. The largest and best organized companies run their own dealing rooms on the analogy of the international banks.

But this overhead, scaled of course to the size and complexity of each company, is normally worth its cost if the sum of the marketing and currency gains outweighs the fixed cost of realizing them.

An important aspect of such an arrangement is that companies with such a system usually net their exposures for the purpose of spot and forward dealing. In the process they save on the banks' dealing margins. If we buy and sell Swedish kronor simultaneously, we pay a margin at both ends. By netting the receipt against the payment, and restricting our exchange deal to the balance, we save this duplication of expense.

As netting cuts down the number of currency deals, it also saves administration costs. This expense can be further reduced by grouping transactions (say) by calendar months. So if we have 900 Swedish kronor transactions falling due in February, of which 600 are receipts and 300 payments, we can wrap them into one forward deal for the net amount instead of taking on the mammoth task of handling hundreds. We looked at the mechanics of netting and synchronization in Chapter 11.

So the classic central matrix system involves (say) monthly printouts from all the sales and purchase accounting centres in the group, showing all the receipts and payments falling due in the next 6 to 12 months or more, one printout for each currency. In these printouts items already covered forward must of course be treated as transactions in the currency for which they have been bought or sold forward, not in the currency in which they are invoiced.

This gives the treasurer the net exposure for each currency and each period. He then decides whether to hedge each such currency/month position not at all, or 25% or 50%, 75% or 100%.

The success of these decisions is then measured, for example by reference to the profit or loss of the central finance company, or by comparing each decision with the outturn of the forward rate against the spot rate on maturity. On this last criterion anything over 50% counts as a success. The total benefit of gains over losses would have to exceed the extra cost of this method as against the second method (accept only selected risks and cover these automatically at birth) in order to justify the extra resources absorbed by this method.

But this criterion of success has two serious shortcomings: First, it takes no account of the marketing effects. The fourth method normally accepts more risks, that is, more sales in currencies other than that of cost, and this must affect volumes and margins. Secondly, it treats the risk management task as a two-horse race between covering forward *today* or waiting for the spot rate on maturity. In fact it is a multihorse race between the rate we can get now and the almost infinite number of rates (many in each hour of dealing) which may be available to us between now and maturity. It is really only if we deal at the best of all those rates that we can truly call ourselves successful. This point is more fully developed in Chapter 23.

CHAPTER 14

Managing Ordinary Trading Risks: Principles

The critical importance of the original pricing decision

This is one of the main recurring themes in our analysis of the nature of trading currency risk, but it is a theme which has not yet received sufficient attention in the literature. The next two chapters will illustrate in more dramatic form how crucial the point is when it comes to large contracts.

But the pricing decisions in more ordinary trading can be just as troublesome. If we issue a price list, we can be committed for a considerable time and for a large volume of relatively small individual sales. Again, if we run a jobbing shop we may make many pricing decisions, but each can be important in its own right in its impact on the profit of the business.

If such a pricing decision involves selling in a currency other than that of cost, it seems essential to make currency expertise available to the decision process. Example 14 illustrates this point for a fairly small transaction.

Example 14   Need for currency expertise in pricing

A manufacturer of table knives in Sheffield has to quote to his French agent for a consignment in French francs. Our planned sterling price is £1000, and we could not accept anything less than £950. The French franc today is quoted spot around Fr9.60 = £1. Payment is 90 days after shipment, but our price to the agent must be kept firm for 14 days before he accepts it. The three months forward rate today is Fr9.51, a premium of 9 centimes. If we could have closed the deal today, a price of Fr9510 could be sold forward for £1000 and give us our desired price. As the competition in this field is hot, we should be ill-advised to quote £1000 at today's spot rate of Fr9.60 = £1, making Fr9600 if the deal were done today. For today we could fix a price without currency risk. It is better to give the customer the benefit of the forward premium than to risk losing the order.

But unfortunately the deal will not be concluded today, and we have to accept and cost for the currency risk of keeping the quotation open for 14 days. So we have to ask: what is the worst that can reasonably happen to the forward rate in 14 days?

The sales manager would probably like to keep the price at Fr9510 (which would be his price for a sale today), hoping that at worst the exchange movement will not cause the sterling proceeds to fall below the rock-bottom minimum of £950. Fr9510 would yield us £950 at Fr10.01 = £1. The question therefore is: could the *forward* rate for three months move any higher than Fr10.01, an increase of 5.26%, in 14 days?

Now the forward rate consists of two elements, the spot rate and the forward premium or discount, and normally the spot rate is by far the most volatile of these. Suppose, for example, that the spot rate moved 5% in favour of sterling to Fr10.08, and the forward premium narrowed at the same time to 5 centimes, then the forward rate would be Fr10.03 in 14 days' time, and a price of Fr9510 would produce less than £950.

The sales manager has got in touch with the treasurer, and together they have identified the need to quote francs, the minimum tolerable sterling price of £950, the importance of the 14-day period, and the need to go for this order in a very competitive market. Now the treasurer may take the view that the franc is behaving less erratically than sterling, that sterling could in fact attract heavy buying if, as seemed likely, OPEC were to announce a further increase in the price of crude oil, and that at the same time a narrowing of the gap between the sterling and franc Eurocurrency interest rates (which would of course reduce the forward premium on the franc) was also on the cards. His view of a reasonable worst case is that in the 14 days the spot rate could go to Fr10.12, coupled with a narrowing of the forward premium to 4 centimes, giving the company a forward rate of Fr10.08. The rock-bottom price should therefore be £950 converted at Fr10.08 = £1, which is Fr9576.

The point of the example is that it is very hard to see how such a decision can be intelligently taken without the advice of someone skilled and experienced in currencies and intimately aware of the state of the currency market.

The example illustrates that currency losses of 5% in a short antenatal exposure period like 14 days are perfectly possible. The conclusion to be drawn from it is not that no pricing decision can ever be taken without the treasurer present, but that decisions to sell in a currency other than that of cost should not be taken without the benefit of such advice whenever the outcome of that particular decision could be material to overall trading performance. And unless pricing decisions are very numerous and fragmented, they may well be of material impact. This is clear from the example of the issue of a price list, but the same applies wherever pricing decisions, or perhaps decisions about minimum selling prices, are taken generically rather than for each individual transaction. In the case where a price list is issued, it may in practice be binding, not legally but commercially, for long periods and for high volumes. Moreover, risk is more sharply geared to the time than to the volume dimension; the longer the interval between the currency judgement and the sale, the greater is the potential currency loss on that sale.

The pricing decision and the fourth method (netting matrix)

In the last chapter we looked at four methods of managing trading risks. The fourth we called the 'to hedge or not to hedge' method or the 'exposure matrix' method. There is no *inherent* reason why a company which adopts that method should not manage trading risks at the point of the pricing decision, but the odds against it are long. A company which practises the exposure matrix system, has all trading risks *collectively* reviewed for each maturity and for each currency, and this seldom leaves room for attention to individual risks. Secondly, the matrix system as such cannot concern itself with risks until they turn up on the matrix, and that is likely to be after the *pricing* decision. This point is self-evident in the case of antenatal risk, which *cannot* be hedged for reasons discussed in Chapter 12; antenatal risk is therefore irrelevant to any 'to hedge or not to hedge' decision. Companies which practise method four often include on the matrix items which are postnatal, but not yet on the balance sheet, and this is obviously the very best practice. But as the risks cannot be antenatal, they will only reach the matrix at the time of the pricing decision in exceptional cases. It takes the coincidence that we have no antenatal period, and that our periodical review happens on the very date that a pricing decision has to be taken, and that the exposure management team happen to be aware of that decision process.

It is therefore fair to conclude that the exposure netting matrix system *as such* does not involve a currency risk management input from the exposure management team into the pricing decision. Such an input may of course occur, but this would be additional to the matrix assessment procedure, and not part of it.

The matrix assessment, therefore, deals with risks which are likely to be (a) postnatal and (b) unhedged at the time of the review. The original pricing decision and the exchange rate used in that decision are likely to be in the category of bygones, and the opportunity to manage the outcome of the trading transaction against that original exchange rate must at this point be regarded as irretrievably lost. *Once we have reached this stage without managing the risk*, the whole approach of the netting matrix and its methodology have become appropriate and valid; by now it has become the best possible practice. It is helpful however to be absolutely clear about the implications:

* The pricing decision was not part of the risk management process.
* Since then the risk has, for whatever period has passed, been in the uncontrolled hands of the market.
* At the point where the risk is managed, it is managed not as an individual risk, but as part of the net exposure in one currency for one maturity.
* This management process is no longer trading risk management, because it is no longer concerned with the rate used in the pricing decision.
* But whereas the *management* process is no longer trading risk management, the transaction itself of course has not changed its char-

acter, and its accounting and tax characteristics are still those of a trading transaction.

It could be objected to this analysis that we do not know how the item will finally go through the exchange market, and that it is perfectly possible for the outcome to be as good or even better than the exchange rate used in the pricing decision. That is obviously true, but if the outturn is no worse than we intended, then we have the market, and not our own management action, to thank.

Real trading risk management, let us repeat, involves two stages. First, currency expertise as an input into the *pricing decision* itself. The currency expert has to give his view on the degree of risk and on the exchange rate to be used for pricing at which the risk is covered or (if it is antenatal) properly costed into the price. Secondly, expertise (mainly dealing skill) is needed to *hedge at birth*, unless there are professional and professionally assessed grounds for leaving the risk unhedged, with the approval of the appropriate authority level.

Once the risk has got past the stage of birth, the netting matrix is a very proper way to manage the risk, as long as it is fully understood that the risk is then no longer being managed as a trading risk, that is, against the original pricing decision, but by now as a *balance sheet* risk. And in that context we shall see in Chapter 19 that this is part of a wider and more general problem than the receivables and payables which started life as trading risks.

The temptations of the netting matrix system

Our conclusion, therefore, is that the netting matrix system is an effective way to deal with trading risks after they have grown up beyond the point where they still are manageable as trading risks, but should merge into balance sheet risk management. We must however look at the temptations into which companies could fall if they have installed the netting matrix system. There are three of them:

1. The temptation to believe that, with such a heavyweight effort at the postnatal stage, there is no need to manage trading risks at the pricing and birth stages. We have amply covered why this is fallacious.
2. The temptation to believe that we are so well equipped to manage them that we can accept risks, that is, sell in currencies other than those of cost, unselectively and without limit. There is even a danger that this will cause us to take on so large a volume of unnecessary risks that we shall find this justifying an even greater overhead to manage them.

3. The temptation to believe that what the matrix nets is what actually neutralizes the original trading risks.

This third and last temptation and fallacy needs to be illustrated by an example.

Example 15   Is netting at maturity enough?

The netting matrix assumes that exposures can be netted as long as they mature simultaneously. As long as we do not believe that this neutralizes true *trading* risks, the assumption evidently holds good.

In this example we are a company in the United States whose sales and costs all arise in dollars, except that when on 1 January 1981 we look at our matrix, we find that on 1 April we are due to receive DM5 million from an export contract signed 1 November 1980, and that also on 1 April 1981 we have to pay DM4 million for a machine ordered 1 June 1980. So far no action has been taken to hedge either D-mark exposure. The netting principle tells us that at 1 April we have a net exposure of DM1 million maturing. If we now sell that DM1 million forward, for example, we have no unhedged exposure left.

Starting from our position on 1 January 1981, all this is obviously true. What is wrong is any assumption that the two risks, therefore, have at all times cancelled one another out, and that our *trading* risk is only a net DM1 million. The company could quite easily already have lost its shirt on *each* of these two transactions, before it attended to the matter on 1 January 1981.

We illustrate this by assuming that the various spot and forward rates stood as follows (dealers' spreads disregarded):

$1 = DM:	1 June 1980	1 November 1980	1 January 1981	1 April 1981
Spot rate	1.95	1.70	1.80	1.80
Forward rate to 1 April 1981	1.96	1.65	1.78	n.a.

If we had bought the D-marks for the machine forward on 1 June when we ordered it, the dollar cost of the machine at DM1.96 would have been $2 040 816. If we had sold the DM5 million receipt forward on 1 November when we signed the contract, it would have produced $3 030 303 at DM 1.65. Our net cash receipt would have been $989 487. If we cover DM1 million forward on 1 Jaunary at DM1.78, we shall realize $561 798. If we fail to cover, the net receipt will at DM1.80 be $555 556. Failure to cover the original risks has cost us $427 689 if we take belated hedging action on 1 January 1981, or $433 931 if we do not.

If we assume that we do cover forward on 1 January and treat the netted receipt and payment as if they had occurred at the actual forward rate of $1.78, then we can allocate the $427 689 loss as follows:

	$
On the machine (DM4 million)	206 375
On the contract receipt (DM5 million)	221 314
	$427 689

For illustration, we have of course taken fluctuations in the rates which produced a substantial loss. The decisions taken could equally have produced a profit. But the fluctuations are well within the swings that occur when the markets are turbulent. The example does not exaggerate the risks taken. It is also realistic in assuming that the dollar is not invariably at a forward discount to the D-mark.

What the example shows quite dramatically, is that if we wish to manage trading risks defensively, we must only net them if they were born with the same exchange rate built into the two pricing decisions. In practice this means they have to be twins, simultaneously conceived. And any hedging action for the balance of receipt over payment (or vice versa) must be taken at their birth. The best place for all this is the maternity ward.

But if we do not wish to manage them defensively at that time, then it is quite valid to treat them subsequently as balance sheet risks and to manage them under that heading.

Our conclusion therefore is that trading risks can only be properly managed as trading risks if attention is given to the currency problem at the time of the pricing decision and at birth when any hedging should be implemented.

One final comment remains to be made. The management effort which goes into the pricing decision must of course be wide-ranging and look at the business decision as a total business decision. If the currency advice at this point is that the risk is very acute and large, and can only be taken with a large currency contingency built into the price, then the team as a whole must review the whole pricing problem and take no previous judgements for granted. For instance, in Example 15, could the German supplier be persuaded to quote a dollar price? Or would it be cheaper to find another supplier who quotes dollars in any case? The currency risk when recognized, may give us a fresh view of how best to buy the machine. Similarly, if we look at the problem of the selling price, if there is an antenatal problem, would it be possible to persuade the customer to settle the final D-mark price at the time of signing the order so as to save both sides the cost of the currency risk? This is a possible solution suggested in the next two chapters when we examine the special problems of large export contracts. But all these judgements and decisions require a closeknit team with combined skills in selling, customer intelligence, purchasing and currency risk management.

CHAPTER 15

Managing Trading Risks of Large Contracts (1)

We are here concerned with contracts for (say) a power station or a civil construction project like a bridge or a dam, or a telecommunication system. Typical terms of payment are 20% down payment with order, 65% against each shipment or monthly certificate of work done, then 10% on handing over the works and the final 5% at the end of a further 12-month warranty period. All this could easily take anything from 2 to 5 years from signature of contract to the collection of the last 5%. Fig. 2 shows a typical cash collection pattern. But the worst currency risk arises not from the length of the total performance and collection period, but from the tender period before the contract is signed. This can take anything from 9 to 18 months.

So we might submit our tender in January of year 1, sign our contract (say) in January of year 2, collect our down payment at that time, then

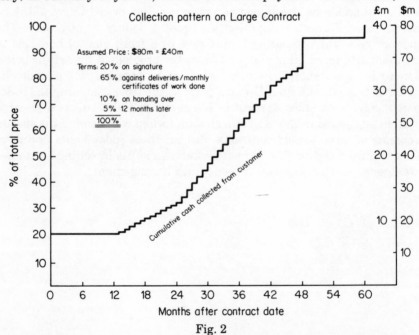

Fig. 2

collect the next 75% over the next 2 to 5 years, that is, at worst up to December of year 6, and the last 5% in December of year 7.

Not only can the periods be very long, but the amounts can be very large, not only in absolute terms, but also as a proportion of our entire annual turnover.

Another characteristic of such contracts is that they often involve sizeable subcontracts. A representative project might have an overall price of £40 million, which includes one £8 million subcontract with a French subcontractor, and £12 million expenditure on local labour, hotel bills, materials all purchased in the local currency of the customer, say in the Middle East.

In the present case we assume that the remaining £20 million represent sterling costs and profit, and that we are a sterling-based company. However, for competitive or other reasons we have had to tender in US dollars. We, therefore, have costs in three currencies and a price in a fourth, unless of course we can persuade the French subcontractor to accept a sterling or (better still) dollar price.

If we priced this large tender on the assumption of £1 = $2, our price would be $80 million.

What is special about large contracts?

Not all such contracts are so large or take so long to perform. Nor are the risks intrinsically different from the other trading risks. But if we take especially the larger contracts of this kind, we find that the problems presented by them are different from those of ordinary trading risks in the following respects:

1. The risks are larger in proportion to the financial characteristics of the company: each risk represents a higher proportion of its equity, its annual profit, its turnover; all of them are nearer, and many of them above the catastrophe level.
2. The time-spans of the risks are longer, and in the currency world the time dimension is all. Even if we believe we can forecast rates for 3 or 6 months ahead, we might be daunted by the task of forecasting 1, 3 or 5 years ahead.
3. The forward markets for most currencies do not stretch to 5 years. For most currencies they stop at 6 or 12 months out.
4. Receipts from customers and payments to subcontractors can be very lumpy, in other words, few and large, so that we can hardly expect to net them against reverse cash flows occurring at or about the same time.
5. While borrowings are a perfectly good hedge against contract receipts in principle, they are rarely found in practice, because borrowings on

82

this scale need to make sense for the capital structure as well as for hedging.
6. Customers often insist on holding bonds against advance payments or performance bonds. If one of these is called, it invalidates our expected phasing of receipts, on the strength of which we have entered into forward contracts.
7. The worst problem by far is the tender period: this risk, usually of considerable duration, can seldom be hedged; it is the most intractable kind of antenatal risk.

If for the moment we leave the last two of these problems aside, we shall find that the others are quite manageable, as long as the currency has a good forward market.

Must hedge when contract has been won

We can take action to hedge the risks as soon as we are sure to have landed our contract. This is usually at signature, sometimes later (if there is real doubt whether the conditions like governmental consents, which are a prerequisite of the contract becoming effective, will be met), sometimes earlier.

At or about that time we should be able to collect our 20% or $16 million down-payment. This leaves us to sell the remaining $64 million forward for the various forward dates on which either the contract or our performance and delivery schedule leads us to *expect* those receipts. In some industries, especially in aircraft exports, it is also common to find terms under which payments or instalments are not geared to proved performance milestones, but are due on predetermined calendar dates. This is of course a great help.

Scope for aggressive management?

There will always be some companies, with a philosophy inclined towards aggressive currency risk management, who would not wish to hedge these risks immediately. They may reflect that their currencies of cost are weaker than the currency of price, and in some cases such a view may well be justified. For our present purposes we shall assume that no risks of this order of magnitude can be tolerated for even an unnecessary day, so that we have the task of hedging the remaining $64 million immediately.

Hedging subcontract payments

The first decision is how the £8 million French franc costs are to be dealt with. Or rather, if we have paid over 20% = £1.6 million on signature, the remaining £6.4 million French franc costs. We have evidently failed to persuade the supplier to accept sterling or dollars. So now we could either buy £6.4 million worth of French francs forward for sterling, or secondly do this for dollars, or buy the French francs spot and deposit them until we need them (this would only be economic if we are in a permanent surplus cash position so that we might as well be depositing in French francs as in some other currency).

There is much to be said in favour of the second alternative of buying francs forward against US dollars. By short-circuiting sterling exchange deals it saves double spreads on the forward deals for that £6.4 million (once on buying francs forward against sterling, and a second time on selling dollars forward against sterling; for the dollar/sterling deal would in that case be reduced from $64 million to $51.2 million). In any case spreads are generally lower for dollar rates than for cross-rates between currencies other than the dollar.

This short-circuiting is obviously very attractive, but could cause difficulty if the forward sales of dollars against francs mature before we need to pay out the francs. Within obvious limits, we might, however, be able to allocate some of the earlier dollar maturities to forward contracts against francs, shifting forward sales of dollars for sterling to later maturities.

Payments in local currency

The £12 million worth of local currency could be more troublesome. It is usually not only in our, but also in the customer's, interest to avoid this exposure by matching, that is, by pricing this element in the local currency. In this helpful case it may be best to take our margins on that local currency portion in our own currency, in other words, to restrict the local currency portion of the contract price to the costs. But this runs the risk of making the non-local supply look expensive.

Where we cannot arrange to take part of the contract price in local currency, there are theoretically the following options open to us in order to hedge the risk:

1. Using forward cover; although quite often the local currency has no adequate forward market;
2. Buying the local currency spot and depositing it in a local bank account until we need it. This can make a large hole in our liquidity

at home. It also exposes the deposit to local exchange controls, present and future, and to a credit risk on the local bank. The amount deposited should be restricted to our known needs, less any accruing interest likely to become available to meet those needs.

Neither of these is likely to be satisfactory in many cases; the lesson is to do our best to negotiate this part of the price in local currency. This should not present too much difficulty.

Uncertain maturities

Tender period and bond risks apart, this leaves the problem of imprecisely known future receipt dates, because many payments in most contracts depend on performance and delivery, both of which are open to the vagaries of human and other hazards, including weather. We can couple with this problem the possibility that the forward market in our particular currency may not stretch as far as the predicted payments. The common result of both problems is that we may have forward contracts which mature before the actual receipts of currency come in from the customer. This is no great problem, especially if the currency of receipt is usually at a forward premium to the currency for which we are selling it forward.

In the present case we are selling dollars forward for sterling, and as long as the dollar is at a forward premium against sterling, we can roll the forward contract over at a gain to the subsequent new maturity date. Rolling over or extending a given forward sale consists of two transactions, closing out the old forward contract spot, and entering into a new one for the new maturity date. In the case of our £40 million = $80 million example, we can do this deliberately with the final 5% payment, if we find that the forward market at the time of signature only extends a maximum of 4 years into the future. We then sell that final payment forward for 4 years, and then roll it over for a final fifth year. The detailed effect of this is illustrated in Example 16.

Example 16

Contract was signed 1 April 1980, and final 5% payment expected 31 March 1985 (5 years later). Longest period for forward contracts on 1 April 1980 was 4 years, so the 5% = $4 million were sold forward on that date at the forward rate of $2.12 for value 31 March 1984, to produce £1 886 792. (The spot rate on 1 April 1980 we assume to have been $2.30 which would theoretically make $4 million = £1 739 130).

We now assume that by 31 March 1984 (a) sterling hardens and (b) sterling weakens from its assumed 1 April 1980 spot and forward rates against the dollar.

(a) On 29 March (we have to deal 48 hours ahead) 1984 the rates are spot $2.50 and forward to 31 March 1985 $2.45.

We have to close out the original forward contract. So we have to buy $4 million spot at $2.50 for £1 600 000. We collect the gain of £1 886 792 − £1 600 000 in cash, producing *£286 792* cash on 31 March 1984.

We now enter into another forward contract selling the $4 million forward to 31 March 1985 at $2.45, to produce a receipt of £1 632 653. This is £109 477 *less* than the original spot equivalent on 1 April 1980 of £1 739 130. The combined result of the two forward contracts is therefore a gain against the original spot rate of £286 792 − £106 477 = £180 315 (plus the interest for the year 1984 on the cash receipt of £286 792). Of the overall gain against the original spot rate (£1 886 792 − £1 739 130 =) £147 662 arose on the first contract for 4 years, and the remaining £32 653 on the second 'rollover' contract for one year.

(b) On 29 March 1984 the spot is $1.90 and the 1-year forward $1.88.

We have to close out by buying $4 million at spot, costing £2 105 263, a loss on the forward price of £1 886 792 amounting to *£218 471*, which we have to pay cash to the bank. The rollover contract at $1.88 will on 31 March 1985 produce £2 127 660, which is *£388 530* better than the original spot of £1 739 130. The net overall result is £388 530 − £218 471 = a gain of *£170 059* (less a year's interest on £218 471). As in (a), £147 662 of this gain is attributable to the first (4-year) forward contract, and the remaining £22 397 to the second 'rollover' contract for 1 year.

So far, then, we have not found any unmanageable problems in these large contracts. As long as we keep away from inconvertible currencies or currencies with no forward markets, our weapons of forward cover and rolling over forward contracts should serve us well from the time we have a contract.

Contract bonds

One of the other two problems is contract bonds. In our example we have a down payment of 20% or $16 million. The customer may well insist on having a 'first demand' (blank cheque) bond against this. This serves as security against our pocketing the $16 million and then forgetting about performance of the contract. The bond is given by a bank in his country; that bank takes an equally unconditional counterindemnity from a bank in our country, which in its turn will want an identical counterindemnity from us.

A bond causes a currency problem if the customer wrongfully 'calls', that is, cashes it, leaving us to pursue our legal rights under the contract to recover the $16 million, plus perhaps the performance bond of (say) $8 million, after much litigation or negotiation. In that case we finally receive many years later that $16 million, which we thought we had received once and for all at the time of signature, and therefore did not cover forward. It may, of course, be that the termination clause in the contract entitles us to recover not only the $16 million, but also interest and any currency loss which we could have suffered if the dollar had meanwhile weakened. But this depends on whether the law of the customer's country, or that of ours, or that of some third country governs the contract and enforces our rights, and finally on whether we can collect our entitlement from our export credit insurers if the arbitration or court award remains unpaid by the customer.

Currency risk is a function of time, and in these large contracts safety lies in being in control of the timetable. Bonds can be a large and gaping hole in that safety-net.

The worst problem: the tender period

This leaves us to look at the worst problem of all: the tender period. The essence of the problem is that we commit ourselves to the price we offer a long time (3, 6 or 9 months are common validity periods) before we know whether we are the selected competitor who will get the contract. Some projects even fail to go ahead altogether when the customer finds out the cost and problems of the project. And if we have no contract, then either exchange controls or our own prudence will forbid us to cover the risk forward. Example 17 illustrates why our own prudence will counsel against such cover.

Example 17

In our example of a $80 million tender, if we decided to cover this forward at the time of tendering, we should be covering forward perhaps some 50 receipts of varying amount, maturing at dates between 1 and 6 years ahead if we assume that the contract is signed within a year of submission of the tender.

On the day we sell forward, the spot rate is $2.10 and the *average* of the 50 forward rates comes to $1.90 = £1. We have therefore sold $80 million forward for £42.11 million, £2.11 million better than our desired sterling price. Now 6 months later we find that our French competitor has won the contract, and we have not. If we now ask the bank to unwind the 50 forward contracts, we find that the spot rate has moved to $1.95 and the average of the forward rates to $1.80, so this will cost us £44.44 million, a cash loss of £2.33 million.

Of course, we can wait hoping for better forward rates, or run the original forward contracts to maturity, but that would be a still greater gamble. No company can afford this magnitude and quality of risk on that majority of its tenders which it is likely to lose. And as we do not know the losing tenders in advance (otherwise we should not incur the large expense of preparing them), it is an inescapable conclusion that we must not hedge tenders.

Example 18   Borrowing dollars instead

If we borrowed dollars instead of selling them forward, the problem would not go away. This may not be obvious if we thought that even if we did not win *this* tender, we were sure to win some dollar tender some time for which we could use our $80 million borrowing. Nor are the main objections that our successful tender might be for a very different amount, or that we are stuck with a large risk to our shareholders' equity in the meantime. No, the worst snag arises from the fact that the $80 million borrowing is no hedge anyway unless we immediately sell the dollars for sterling, presumably at the spot rate of $2.10, producing £38.1 million. When we realize that we have lost our tender, we could repay this by paying out £41.0 million at $1.95 = £1 (losing £2.9 million in cash). But we have decided not to do this and to wait for the next successful tender. Let us say we have the luck that the successful tender is for $80 million. But at what exchange rate did we compute our price of £80 million for this successful tender? This rate may well have been $1.78, in which case our desired sterling price was £45 million, and our initial borrowing only produced £38.1 million, resulting in a disastrous loss of £6.9 million. But why did we not simply convert our £45 million price at $2.10 to give us a dollar price of $94.5 million, of which $80 million were covered by the borrowing? Presumably because with the dollar at $1.78 our price of $94.5 million would be uncompetitive, especially against any UK competitors. (*Note*: in this example we have ignored the spread between the bank's buying and selling rates and the difference between sterling and dollar interest rates.)

We, therefore, have to conclude that we cannot hedge the tender period risk by the usual methods of forward cover or currency borrowing without taking on board worse exposures than we tried to manage in the first place.

How can we manage the tender period risk?

So what can be done about the tender period risk? Broadly we can deal with it in five possible ways:

1. Avoid the exposure by quoting in the currency or currencies of cost. Even multicurrency tenders have before now been won. This is the ideal answer, but unfortunately in the case at which we are looking, this would disqualify our tender from the customer's consideration, under his conditions in the invitation to tender.
2. There are rare instances where governmental insurance schemes are available against this risk. In the United Kingdom the 'tender to contract' cover is offered by the Export Credits Guarantee Department, but only in those special cases in which the ECGD's conditions are met. There is a brief description of the scheme at the end of this chapter.
3. If the customer's conditions permit, we can tender in dollars at a price of $80 million, but specify that this price will vary up or down *pro*

rata to $\dfrac{AFR}{2.00}$, where *AFR* is the weighted average of the forward rates at which we shall be able to sell the dollars forward on the date of signature of the contract, and 2.00 is the rate at which we did in fact convert our tender price from sterling into dollars. The customer may find it attractive that in return for his acceptance of the currency risk in the tender period we offer him the full benefit of the forward premium on the dollar.*

4. In many cases the solution in 3 above will also be found to break the customer's conditions laid down for the tender. In that case it should nevertheless be offered as a non-compliant, but optional alternative to the not very attractive remaining solution in 5 below. It can surely not be wrong to offer the customer an extra option. It will certainly be a more competitive option if properly evaluated.

5. Finally we have to face the difficult and thankless task of calculating what contingency needs to be built into the conversion rate so as to protect us against a large loss through adverse currency movements in the tender period. We have to do this because we can neither hedge nor avoid the risk. If we are left with this tough case, it is very important to specify the shortest possible validity period for the price of the tender—the longer the period, the worse is the risk. The evaluation of the contingency is one of the most difficult judgements a treasurer has to make. His task is to assess at what rate the price will safely protect the desired proceeds in the currency of cost without making the tender unnecessarily uncompetitive. He must do justice to the fact that uncertainty is one of the worst costs in business, and that the tender period currency risk is one of the worst uncertainties. Suppose today's spot rate is \$2.10 = £1 and the tender has a minimum validity of 6 months. Suppose further that the rate has never been known to rise by more than 10% in any past period of 6 months, and we have no reason to think that the next 6 months could get worse than the worst past experience. We might then be able to justify an assumed worst spot rate of 110% of \$2.10, viz \$2.31 = £1. We next have to assess what is the least favourable weighted average forward premium for the spectrum of forward periods from date of contract to dates of receipts for this tender. The forward premium has in fact on rare occasions* been negative for the dollar/sterling rate, but it would not be reasonable to assume that this could recur after a steep rise of sterling from \$2.10 to \$2.31. If the average forward period were about 2½ years, we might assess the worst (in this case the smallest) average forward premium at 2½%, giving us a worst-case conversion rate of 97½% of \$2.31 = \$2.2522. If, as we assumed at the beginning

---

*Since the above section was written in 1980, the dollar has been at a forward discount against sterling for a considerable period.

of Chapter 15, we want to safeguard a sterling price of £40 million, this implies a dollar price of $90 088 000. This will horrify our colleagues in sales management. They may then of course review whether they really need £40 million, but that is not a currency problem but a commercial problem. The calculation is of course only an illustration, but it shows how we could reasonably justify this substantial increase in the required dollar price, just because we cannot sell forward when we tender. And all this assumed that we are free to change our price after 6 months. If there is any genuine doubt on legal or commercial grounds about our ability to do that, then we might have to add an even greater contingency. On the other hand, if we had been able to restrict the validity period to 4 months, we should have arrived at a substantially lower contingency against the tender period currency risk. No wonder therefore that we find it advisable to add in the extra option of a currency adjustment clause coupled with a substantially lower dollar price, which we recommended in 4 above!

Default by the customer

This antenatal risk in the tender period is the worst of the currency risks in the field of large export contracts. It should not however be forgotten that if we have sold receipts forward or if we have costs in third currencies, any default or late payment by the customer will carry with it further currency risks. In some cases these can be recovered from export credit insurers like the Export Credits Guarantee Department in the United Kingdom. This is reasonable as the loss from this exposure would after all be a consequence of the insured default by the customer. But whether we have credit insurance cover or not, it is important to make sure that our contract conditions entitle us to recover such currency losses from the customer, especially in the event that the contract is terminated on the grounds of his breach.

It is also worth mentioning that credit insurance cover is often restricted to a total limit calculated in the exporter's currency. If therefore the amount of the contract price rises in terms of that currency as a result of a rise in the contractual currency against it, there is a risk that this will reduce the adequacy of the credit insurance cover.

But none of these problems are in the same league as the tender period for causing treasurers to age prematurely.

Appendix: The 'tender to contract' cover offered by the Export Credits Guarantee Department of the United Kingdom: short summary

Availability

* The cover is available only for export contracts from the United Kingdom denominated in US dollars or D-marks.
* For a contract to qualify, its UK content must be £5 000 000 or more.
* The cover is available for ECGD-supported buyer credits and supplier credits or cash contracts insured under ECGD specific type credit insurance guarantees.
* The cover was originally designed to protect UK exporters against currency risks into which they were forced by the 'switch' policy adopted in December 1976 under which buyer and supplier credits normally had to be financed in dollars or D-marks. It was, however, also made available for cash contracts. When the switch policy was abandoned in March 1980, the facility remained available for contracts in dollars and D-marks, which ECGD continues to encourage.

Cost

Each *tender* attracts a flat charge of £5000. If the tender is successful, a further charge is payable to ECGD on receipt of down payment. The charge varies with the period for which the guaranteed exchange rates used to prepare the tender are valid. The maximum validity period is 9 months, for which the charge is 1.05% of guaranteed receipts.

How the cover works

The exporter may apply for TTC cover at any time before tendering but at the latest will be required to make a commitment shortly after ECGD's first indication of the availability of buyer credit support or supplier credit insurance. In his application for TTC cover the exporter nominates a date for receiving ECGD's guaranteed forward exchange rates based on his estimate of when he will be required to commit himself to a firm currency price. On receipt of those rates he must pay the initial premium of £5000. If the tender is successful then shortly before contract signature the exporter prepares a schedule of the amounts and timing of expected currency receipts. By reference to the appropriate guaranteed rates he can calculate the guaranteed sterling outturn for those currency amounts. On contract signature the exporter enters into forward sales for the currency amounts and period shown on his schedule.

Financial outcome of the cover

The extent of any payments by ECGD to the exporter, or vice versa, depends on the difference between the guaranteed sterling amounts shown on the schedule and the sterling actually received when the currency receipts are surrendered for sterling under the forward contracts. The effects of rolling-over (extending) the forward contracts because of later receipt of currency than was assumed in the schedule are also fully taken into account when calculating the sterling actually received by the exporter. If the difference between such actual sterling outturn and the guaranteed sterling outturn results in a gain, ECGD is entitled to the first 10% of the gain and the exporter to the balance. If the result is a loss, the exporter bears the first 1½% and any excess over 25%, but ECGD makes good to the exporter any losses within the 1½% to 25% band. In the last two sentences the percentages (10%, 1½%, 25%) are all calculated on the guaranteed sterling outturn for the total currency received to date. The cumulative position is reviewed each month and any settlement made a month later.

CHAPTER 16

Managing Trading Risks of Large Contracts (2)

Having described the trading risks of large contracts in Chapter 15, we now have to address the principles involved.

Large contracts more than any other form of trading illustrate that trading exposures are not just a matter of assets and liabilities on the balance sheet at any point of time. The worst exposures are *tenders*, which may never become transactions of the business at all. Consequently they cannot be on the balance sheet. But even *after* signature of a contract, the commitment to make and sell will not reach the balance sheet until it turns up in the form of stock or receivables or payables or advance payments, and only this last item will appear at or about the time of signature. As these are likely to rank among a company's worst currency risks, this alone is a telling reason why we must describe trading risks as a mismatch between currencies of price and costs, not in terms of assets and liabilities.

Can we manage these risks aggressively?

Perhaps the biggest issue is whether this field of large export contracts is one in which there is any room for aggressive currency risk management policies. Or, to drop the euphemism, for taking contracts in unmatched currencies and deliberately leaving the exposure open in the expectation of a large currency gain. Anyone who has watched the rise of sterling against the dollar by over 50% between December 1976 and November 1980, will no doubt think that any company in the United Kingdom should question its corporate sanity if it even contemplated such a policy. But sterling had its steep slide from January 1975 to December 1976, losing a third of its dollar parity in under 2 years, and during that period all the pundits among the commentators in the press, and some authorities in more responsible positions, criticized UK exporters for not accepting precisely these exposures by selling in dollars or other 'hard' currencies and using the 'inevitable' gains to hedge against the ravages of UK inflation! And under the pressure of this considerable and powerful lobby quite a few companies switched to tendering in dollars without attempting to hedge the risks; after all, any such hedge would have undone the 'cover' against inflation!

The concept of selling in currencies other than the currency of cost is perfectly sound with ordinary export transactions if the reasoning is that the customer will pay a better sterling price to the UK exporter if the price is expressed in dollars *and covered forward* than if the price is expressed in sterling. We considered this point in Chapter 13.

But in the case of large contracts the policy runs into the enormous problem of the tender period risk. In the sterling slide of 1975–76 the idea of selling in non-sterling currencies did not really catch on until well into 1977. Any tenders submitted after that might well have become contracts well after sterling had begun its long climb back from around $1.60 towards $2.40, and many of those contracts must have been taken at a currency loss.

In any case, a more cautious policy is of course to make a strict rule that all contract currency risks must be hedged at the time of signature. This leaves the problem of the tender period on one side for the moment. But once we have failed to cover forward at the time of signature, we are presumably committed to the view that sterling will slide again and give us a better result if we cover forward at some more favourable future date. But even if sterling did oblige us and dipped, when exactly is it our policy to cover forward? Presumably the answer is at the trough, but how do we know when the trough comes? How do we then distinguish between a temporary rally and a change of trend? Is this not precisely why all stock market operators are not millionaires? And are these the kind of risks that company managements should take with large amounts? And as we await the trough, will not some receipts come in from the customer in the meantime at currency rates which we have failed to manage and which may therefore be very unfavourable to us? Donaldson (1980) makes the point very clearly: 'Between the time at which an exposure arises and the time at which it matures the currency required to settle the underlying transaction must be bought or sold. No matter how volatile the market, there must always be an optimum moment at which to make the deal.'

But none of the practitioners have solved that conundrum. Not only would there be a considerable cost in monitoring the optimum moment *after the event*, but at the time it would take a genius to recognize it. It is therefore reasonable to conclude that *postnatal* risks are not acceptable in this field. The time-spans and the amounts are such that we should, in prudence, make it a rule that all exposures must be hedged as soon as the award of the contract is a legal or commercial certainty, and no later.

The anatenatal risk of the tender period

If we can conclude that postnatal risks in this field must not be under-taken voluntarily, we are left with the *antenatal* problem of the tender period.

In the last chapter we saw that the real issue in the tender period is whether we:
1. refuse to accept the risk and quote currencies of cost only,
2. disguise that refusal by qualifying the exposed currency price with a currency adjustment clause,
3. accept the risk but try to protect it by quoting a high and possibly uncompetitive price, converted at a rate which contains a large con-tingency against adverse currency movements,
4. proceed as in 3 but offer a currency adjustment clause as a further, probably cheaper alternative to the customer.

In both 2 and 4 the adjustment clause would give the customer any benefit of the forward rates as an extra inducement for shouldering the tender period risk. In the special cases where insurance against the risk is possible, for example under the ECGD 'tender to contract' cover in the United Kingdom, this dilemma does not arise.

What should a company's approach be to these alternatives? The risks are so large and severe in so many cases that most companies will explore every avenue to see whether they can get the contract without accepting the risk. In the case of a purely formal open tender, where any deviation from the rigid conditions set by the customer disqualifies the tenderer, the choice is between accepting the risk at the unattractive price or adding the optional extra, which should in most cases be permissible. The purely formal set of rules is not particularly fair if some tenderers have their costs in the required currency. Those lucky ones have the unfair advantage of being free from the heavy burden of the tender period risk.

All other tender situations vary from case to case, and there may be opportunities to negotiate out of the risk by being allowed to quote the currencies of cost or to quote the currency adjustment clause up to the date of signature. If we can do this, then we certainly should. For if this risk cannot be equitably passed to the customer in return for other concessions, then international trade in this contract field will suffer.

Conflict between commercial objectives and financial prudence

If we cannot escape from the dilemma, that is, if we must shoulder the risk or do without the contract then we come down to the usual business problem of how badly we need the contract. Ultimately we must be willing to accept some unpalatable burdens if we badly need the orders. Even then a very thin, but safe, margin is better than a large risk which might leave us with a negative margin (sometimes known as a loss).

Need for professional assessment and top level decisions

These are agonizing decisions, but whenever the size of the risk is large, it is clear that the risk itself must be professionally and objectively valued by expert staff, and the decision taken at the appropriate high level in the company. In most companies this would be at the level of the parent board or chief executive, who after all are answerable for this order of risk to the owners of the company.

Very weak currency of cost

In this chapter we have assumed that there is a significant chance of a really catastrophic level of loss if the risk should turn sour. It is perhaps conceivable that the exporter has his costs in such a weak currency that almost any exposure is likely to be profitable. At first sight this situation would be one in which a more aggressive policy would be justifiable. In practice, however, such an exporter would find that his problem takes the form of an almost unlimited range of possible cost inflation rates. One has in mind a contractor operating from a base in Brazil for example. He would then have to ask himself whether he can *safely* assume that the rate of cruzeiro devaluation against the currency of sale will at no time fall behind the internal cost inflation index. This is an even more tantalizing problem. If the exporter does not wish to take a chance on this, he has to offer the customer an even more complex price formula than his competitor in a country like the United Kingdom.

Reference

Donaldson, J. A. (1980), *Corporate Currency Risk*, The Financial Times Business Information Ltd., London, chapter 4, pp. 68–70.

CHAPTER 17

Managing Risks from Intragroup Transactions

Does intragroup trading cause currency risk?

Whether intragroup sales are a source of currency risk *to the group* has been much debated. The principle can be illustrated by an example.

Example 19   Indirect export selling

A German manufacturer sells a product to the United States. He wants to receive DM12 000 per item in Germany. A local distributor needs another 50% on top of that for his costs and margin. On the assumption of $1 = DM2.00 this makes a buying cost from Germany of $6000 = DM12 000, and a selling price to the ultimate customer of $9000. In the extreme case where the transfer price to the distributor was agreed on the telephone while on another telephone line the US distributor is arranging the D-mark remittance, there is no currency risk because there is no time-lag during which the currency can move adversely. Failing such unusual synchronization, there is a risk. If the price is agreed at $6000, the German exporter carries the risk; if at DM12 000, then the US distributor has the risk. Either side can, of course, hedge it by forward cover.

Now if we replace the distributor with a subsidiary of the German company in the United States, the position is not changed in either country. If the intercompany price is fixed in dollars, the German parent has the risk; if in D-marks, then the US subsidiary has it, unless once again they agreed the price at a rate at which one of them was simultaneously doing the exchange deal. Again, the one with the risk can of course cover it forward, but the debate is about whether the group as a whole *has* a risk to cover forward.

If we assume that the payment to the German parent has not been covered forward, and the rate moves to $1 = DM1.80, then one party or the other will have a loss. If the intercompany price was fixed in dollars, the $6000 will only produce DM10 800. The parent company has lost DM1200. The US company is not affected, and DM1200 is the group loss from the movement in the exchange rate. If on the other hand the intercompany price was in D-marks, the subsidiary now has a cost of $6667; it has made a currency loss of $667. The parent is all square this time, so the group loss from the currency movement is $667 = DM1200. It has been objected that this loss need not occur because the subsidiary should theoretically be able to recoup or avoid this loss by raising its price to the outside customer by this $667. If this contention were correct, then of course there would be no risk in the indirect selling arrangement from currency movements.

96

The example has therefore brought out the issues needed to clarify the dispute. The answer to the objection is that:

1. The price increase would in any case be impossible if the subsidiary had already entered into its own contract of sale before the currency rate moved.
2. The ultimate customer will only pay the higher price if market conditions give him no better alternative, for example, if the German product has a monopoly and the demand for it is so intense that customers will buy it at virtually any price.

In the latter case we could use economic jargon and say that the subsidiary could raise the price if the elasticity of demand for the goods were zero, a very rare condition in the market. And if this were the case, should we not have raised the price without waiting for the D-mark to rise? The fact that prices cannot be raised in this manner in the normal course of things, is borne out by all the experience of J-curves and the sluggishness of price responses to currency changes.

We are bound, therefore, to dissent from the proposition that intra-group sales do not give rise to currency risks. The idea tends to take hold where trading risks are seen in terms of assets and liabilities, rather than in terms of costs and prices. But even in balance sheet terms it is clear that an exposure is created by the sale. It is of course self-evident that internal current account balances cancel out on consolidation. But the real risk here arises because the *group*, viewed collectively, has its costs in D-marks and sells in dollars. If we put it in those terms, it is the most classical of trading risks. What can be different is that in many such cases there are two separate pricing decisions involved. The internal transfer price is agreed first, and the US subsidiary then makes a separate decision at a different time about its selling prices to external customers. Indeed it may revise those decisions from time to time if it buys in D-marks and the D-mark/dollar rate fluctuates. In this situation the currency exposure arises in the US company between its internal buying price and its external selling price. If the transfer is in US dollars, then the risk arises in the German company between its cost and its dollar selling price.

If we want to describe this risk in balance sheet terms, it is not the internal current account balance which gives rise to the risk, but the asset which begins as German inventory, and after a stage of being US inventory becomes a US receivable and then dollar cash. When it becomes a receivable, the gain or loss crystallizes, unless of course the transfer price is in dollars, in which case it crystallizes when the internal balance becomes a receivable to the German company.

Intragroup sales therefore involve the same risk for the *group* as would be borne *jointly* by the two sides to the internal transfer if they were not

98

members of the same group. Between them they have a risk unless they have synchronzied their transfer price decision with the currency deal. The party which is not dealing in its own currency, carries the risk. If that party manages the risk to its own best advantage, it will also manage it to the best advantage of the group, for its risk is identical with the group exposure.

All this is subject to the effect of tax. If a gain or loss arises, and if the two companies have different marginal rates of tax, then the group will not be indifferent to which of them has the gain or loss.

Do intragroup loans and other balances cause currency risk?

Example 20   US parent finances Italian subsidiary

An American parent company holds purely nominal equity in an Italian subsidiary, and lends it $10 000 so that the Italian company can invest in a lire-denominated redeemable bond worth Lit8 million. The spot rate was Lit800 = $1, so that the loan produced Lit8 million cash. A month later the lira collapses to Lit900 = $1. The subsidiary hastily borrows Lit9 million from its bank and repays the parent company loan.

The position is now as follows:

	Month 1 $	Month 2 $
US parent		
Loan to subsidiary	10 000	
Cash repaid by subsidiary		10 000
Italian subsidiary		
Redeemable bond Lit8 million, translated	10 000	8889
Loan from parent Lit8 million	(10 000)	–
Owed to bank Lit9 million		(10 000)
Consolidated net group position	$10 000	$8 889

(As the bond is a monetary asset its translation at the closing exchange rate is free from controversy.)

The example shows that the Italian subsidiary has suffered a currency loss of Lit1 million, which at Lit900 = $1 is the equivalent of $1111. And that is also the loss to the group. But was this loss due to the intragroup loan? Well, it is obviously arguable in this example that the loss was entirely due to the refinancing of the intercompany debt by borrowing Lit9 million from the bank. So it was the Italian company's liability of $10 000 which caused the loss. But if we look at the consolidated net position and its make-up, the loan in month 1 cancelled out at the identical figure of $10 000, and the group loss in month 2 is due to the fact that the value of the bond in terms of dollars has dropped by

$1111. And this latter theory can be reinforced by pointing out that the result would have been the same if the purchase of the bond had been financed from an external borrowing of dollars. So we appear to have a difficulty in determining whether the loan did or did not cause the loss.

For the answer we must go back to our definition of balance sheet risk. Balance sheet gains or losses result from having more assets than liabilities in one currency or vice versa. The loss to the group resulted from using dollars to finance the purchase of the bond, and it does not matter whether it was the parent or the subsidiary that raised the dollars. The intercompany loan *as such* did not cause the loss. If the US parent had borrowed Eurolire to finance the loan to the Italian subsidiary, the group would incur no loss. What matters are the external assets and liabilities of the group.

Leading and lagging

We looked at leading and lagging in Chapter 11, because it is popularly discussed as a hedging device. We must briefly review it again here because it is an important aspect of the problems and opportunities of intercompany transactions within a group of companies.

Leading and lagging is the deliberate lengthening or shortening of intragroup credit. It is not essentially relevant to trading risks as we have defined them, because the essence of trading risks in our sense is that they are a threat to the assumptions built into a *pricing* decision. Leading and lagging is a device normally applied to whatever trade credit is currently in force, irrespective of whether the pricing decisions lie in the past or in the future. It is, as we said, essentially a device for manipulating the balance sheet.

It is most often used to shift the balance of net assets towards what are believed to be strong currencies or away from weak currencies. By definition, this implies (a) that we know which currencies will be weaker or stronger, or have reasonable grounds for believing that our judgement in the matter is correct, and (b) that our views on this have just undergone a change, for otherwise our previous credit periods would not have needed changing.

This last is, of course, an aggressive form of currency risk management, because it is not designed to neutralize risk but to shift the risk towards what in our judgement is a more favourable configuration of assets and liabilities in the currencies affected. Even if we shift the risk away from a weak currency, this is not defensive management. The latter would be involved if we used leading and lagging towards the point at which our exposure in the currencies reaches neutrality, that is, where assets equal liabilities in each currency except the parent currency.

Not only is such use of leading and lagging rare in practice, but it is also impeded by many constraints. These are mainly exchange controls: at the time of writing this in 1980, French companies are penalized if they accept more than 12 months credit from associated companies, and Italian companies must not give more than 6 months credit. Other constraints come from the fact that trade credit can seldom be negative, and that external borrowings to replace trade credit may not be available.

Leading and lagging became popular in the 1960s, in what we now know were the dying stages of the Bretton Woods era. In those days it was not difficult to spot a weak currency; it was any currency with a more than transient balance-of-payments deficit. The classical example was sterling. As currencies were not floating, the authorities could in the short term only raise interest rates or arrange borrowings from the IMF or other central banks to 'defend' the currency (meaning the official rate). Such a policy could either succeed or fail. If it failed, there was a devaluation of a major order by floating system standards, say by at least 10% or 15%. If it succeeded, market operators could be absolutely confident that the currency could not rise. It could either stay put or fall. In those circumstances any prudent treasurer would do what he could to reduce his net asset position in that currency, because he could not lose. At worst he would not gain in terms of principal, although he might well be paying higher interest rates for weak than for alternative strong currency funds (more about that below). In these circumstances treasurers had an opportunity to pursue a *safe* aggressive policy. That option generally does not exist in a floating regime. It is hard to find a situation in which leading and lagging action does not have a significant chance of losing on the principal amount of funds switched from a supposedly weak to a strong currency.

Bearing in mind therefore the constraints of exchange control, of amounts available as balances, and of funds available in the weaker currency to replace the intragroup credit, and bearing in mind the risk of being wrong, it is not surprising that leading and lagging is met less frequently in practice, and hardly ever as a truly defensive device to neutralize the balance sheet risk on particular currencies.

We cannot leave this topic without discussing the interest and tax effects of using it. The great need, here and elsewhere, is to warn against the interest trap.

Example 21

A French company in the group regularly sells to the Swiss group company, giving 120 days credit. On average the credit balance outstanding to France is FF250 000 = Swiss Fr100 000. The credit is financed by the French banks at 13%, whereas in Switzerland credit costs 6½%. The rates in each case are those for the domestic currency. Should the group arrange for the French company to

withdraw trade credit from the Swiss company so as to save a net (13% − 6½%
=) 6½% of Swiss Fr100 000 (or of FF 250 000) per annum?

Well, the track record is that the Swiss franc does rise against the French
franc at an average rate in excess of 6½% per annum, that the interest differential of 6½% is not a reliable permanent feature, and that in any case the effect
of tax may well be that a loss on the principal will outweigh an equivalent pretax
gain on interest in the group. The company casualty list is full of companies
which have fallen for this interest trap by borrowing low-cost Swiss franc or D-
mark funds, only to find that they ended up with a mountainous repayment
obligation (in terms of their home currencies) which they could not meet.

Finally, there is the after-tax effect of leading and lagging as a whole.
By transferring borrowings and therefore interest burdens from one
country to another, the group shifts profit from the latter to the former,
and this can affect its consolidated tax burden. In which direction the
tax burden is affected, up or down, depends on the marginal tax rate of
each of the group companies involved in the leading and lagging operation. This point clearly needs attention. It should, however, be added
that groups of companies will find it advantageous to act as good corporate citizens in all countries where they operate. Purely artificial action
to switch funds or profit across frontiers can be treated as tax avoidance
in some countries, and in others it can lead to less tangible but still
important disadvantages.

Intercompany dividends, royalties, interest and management charges

It is doubtful whether the currency implications of these items are their
primary characteristics. All of them give rise to well-known tax problems. Some countries restrict payment of them by exchange controls,
some by penal taxation. Royalties, interest and management charges are
often disallowed as expenses reducing taxable profits. In addition all of
them, dividends above all, are often the subject of withholding taxes.
Even after double tax relief, groups of companies are often worse off as
a result of these purely internal transactions. And yet they can play a
very important part in replenishing a group parent company's cash resources and shareholders' funds.

A group can make large profits outside its home country, boosted
perhaps by not bearing their fair share of the central managing and
financing overhead; it may then be under pressure to pay out dividends
geared to its *consolidated* worldwide profit cover. Such a group will tend
to exhaust its domestic cash resources and parent company reserves
unless it repatriates a commensurate part of its foreign subsidiaries'
profits by one or other of these routes.

In comparison with these tax, liquidity and dividend cover problems, the currency aspects of these internal profit streams into the parent company are likely to be of minor importance.

Meanwhile, from the point of view of currency risk *management*, these transactions are not essentially trading risk problems, because they rarely involve any pricing decisions. As in the case of leading and lagging, we must clearly recognize that the transactions are *revenue* rather than capital for tax and accounting purposes, but in currency risk management terms, they involve the techniques and decision processes of balance sheet rather than trading risk management.

Each of these dividends or royalties, etc., involves two stages, the book entry (declaration of dividend, charging of royalty, debiting of interest or management charge) which creates an intercompany balance, and its discharge by cash payment. The first leg, the accounting debit, reduces the shareholders' funds in the paying company and increases those in the recipient. It therefore represents a shift in the *currency* breakdown of the consolidated net worth. More equity is now in the parent currency and less in the currency of the paying company.

The currency exposure of the group is of course unaffected by this first leg of the intercompany transaction; this will only occur after the second leg, the remittance. But the first stage (the book entry) has changed the currency balance in one of the two companies. In the case of a dividend, which is presumably denominated in the currency of the subsidiary, the parent company has acquired a receivable in that currency which it may wish to manage by hedging. If the transaction is a management charge, it may well be denominated in the currency of the parent, in which case the subsidiary has acquired a liability in the parent currency which it may wish to manage during the interval until remittance. And the remittance will change the currency portfolio of the group as a whole. If it is a remittance from Italian subsidiary to French parent, it makes the group shorter of lire and longer of French francs.

If the group has any element of choice about these transactions and their timing, then it has an opportunity similar to the leading and lagging opportunity, of using these transactions so as to improve its balance sheet risk position in the desired direction. It is obviously a limited opportunity, and it arises only if, for example, it is free to get the subsidiary in country X to declare a dividend or to accelerate or delay its remittance, without overriding exchange control, tax or dividend cover and liquidity constraints on that freedom. Like leading and lagging, it is an opportunity to shift the currency balance of the group towards what is believed to be stronger currencies or towards zero balance in the currencies concerned. The former would be aggressive, and the latter defensive currency risk management.

Centralized or decentralized management of risks?

In this chapter we have concluded that where one group company (for example, the French parent) sells into another country (say Italy) through a group selling company in that country, one of the two group companies, the Italian or the French, will have a trading currency risk identical with the risk carried by the group as a whole. And the company with the risk is the one whose currency is not the currency of the intercompany transfer price. If the price is determined in lire, then the French parent has the risk, if in francs, then the Italian subsidiary has it. As long as we have this identity of interest between the company at risk and the group, there is no inherent reason in principle why the Italian subsidiary should not manage the risk, for example, by covering it forward. The action does not have to be central, although the company centre may well wish to lay down policy, such as that all risks should, in the absence of a special dispensation, be hedged.

We found that all other intercompany transactions, including those of intercompany dividends, royalties, interest and management charges, are best regarded as balance sheet problems. Here we concluded that in each case what matters is the consolidated position of the whole group, and this must necessarily be managed centrally. No one foreign subsidiary has the facts at its disposal, because its own position is unlikely to be identical with that of the group. This balance sheet problem is a collective one for the group, whereas the trading problem is strictly a separate one for each and every pricing decision.

In which currency should we invoice intercompany indirect sales?

So far we have taken a neutral view whether the French parent company should invoice its Italian subsidiary in francs or in lire. The financial risk can be hedged either way. If it is francs, the Italian company can buy them forward. If it is lire, the French company can sell them forward. Our choice may of course be influenced by practical factors; either Paris or Milan may have exchange control restrictions or a less efficient forward currency market. But these are not matters of principle.

But if we are correct in believing that the heart of the trading risk is in what happens to our pricing decisions, then we ought to pay some attention to where the pricing decision is taken. We are assuming that the goods go from the French parent (with French franc costs) via the Italian subsidiary to customers in Italy who pay in lire.

Where are the Italian final prices decided? Let us first assume that they are decided by the marketing director of the Italian company. The spot rate is Lit200 = Fr 1, and the intercompany price is Fr 250 per unit, which costs the Italian company Lit50 000. It marks this up to Lit60 000 so as to have a minimum gross margin of $16^2/_3$% on the selling price.

Now let us suppose that the rate changes to Lit160 = Fr 1. This reduces the purchase cost to the Italian company from Lit50 000 per unit to Lit40 000. The Italian company finds itself with a doubled markup of Lit20 000 per unit. This may be just as well, if it previously had some difficulty making ends meet with a margin of only Lit10 000. But it could be that the Italian company considers that it would rather use the windfall cost reduction to reduce its selling prices so as to get extra sales and market share. If this is a very competitive and price-sensitive market, then it will almost certainly choose this course of action even if its marketing director has never read about demand elasticity in an economics textbook. Again, the decision may be to adopt a halfway position and to use just part of the saving for a price reduction and to increase the profit margin with the remainder.

The important point here is that none of this may happen if the intercompany price is fixed in lire. Theoretically the French company may be alive to the marketing decision facing the Italians, and therefore compensate the currency movement by reducing its lire price to the Italian company, but this is not really likely. The difference is that the Italian company can hardly fail to notice the dramatic improvement in its buying costs if it carries the exposure by buying in francs, whereas the French company is unlikely to spot the marketing opportunity in Italy if it carries the currency exposure; it is much more likely to pocket the extra margin without further thought.

If on the other hand the Italian domestic prices to outside customers are decided by the marketing director of the French company, then he is more likely to be alerted to the opportunity in Italy if the French company carries the currency exposure by invoicing in lire. This is of course a much less common organization structure. It is much more common to find that the pricing decisions are taken in the country where the goods are sold to outside customers, in this case Italy.

To sum this up, the question of which is the best currency for intercompany invoicing is probably more closely related to economic than to financial currency risk. Human nature being what it is, the way to make sure that pricing decisions are taken in the best and most beneficial manner is to place the currency exposure with that company in the group which has the task of determining the ultimate selling price to an outside customer. And the most beneficial pricing decision is the one which optimizes the tradeoff between margin and volume. On this point we must part company with those who object that the best pricing decision is always to charge the highest price which the market will bear. This ignores the volume aspect of the pricing decision, and in price-sensitive goods that is the critical part of the decision. Costs are not immaterial to economic decision-taking.

It would, of course, be wrong to claim that no other factors should enter into the choice of currency for intercompany trading, but in practice the benefit of enabling pricing decisions to be taken with immediate knowledge of the currency aspects of cost is likely to outweigh the other factors.

PART 5

Managing and Identifying Balance Sheet Risk

CHAPTER 18

What Assets and Liabilities are Part of the 'True' Balance Sheet Risk?

At the end of Chapter 5 we provisionally defined balance sheet risk as any imbalance of net assets in any one non-reporting currency. That provisional definition tacitly assumes:

* that every item on the balance sheet counts towards that risk;
* that no items which are not on the balance sheet form part of the risk; and
* that the accounting values necessarily constitute a correct measure of the risk.

We must now question these assumptions. For this purpose we postulate a concept of 'true' risk which is independent of the accounting conventions in all these three respects. We do not rule out that 'true' and accounting risk can be identical in any of these respects, but that remains to be seen.

We use the word 'true' rather than 'real' or 'economic', because in this book we use 'real' in the sense of inflation-adjusted, and 'economic' in the marketing sense set out in Chapter 3.

An illustration may help. Suppose we believe that only monetary assets and liabilities are effectively exposed to risk from currency movements (a belief which inspires some supporters of the temporal method of translation), and we have some yen assets and liabilities in our company in Germany, and that we wish to protect our company against the risk of yen/D-mark movements. We must then ascertain our net monetary assets denominated in yen, and borrow that amount of yen for the respective lifespans in our business of those yen items. We ignore all the non-monetary items because we start with the belief that they are not part of our risk.

The task therefore is one of (a) identifying, and (b) valuing the assets and liabilities which make up our true risk, irrespective of the accounting answers to those questions. And we first address ourselves to the task of identification. What we are asking in this chapter is whether various classes of assets or liabilities could represent a risk to the true net worth of the company if there were an adverse movement between the currency in which we hold them and the reporting currency. It is worth reiterating

109

that we may be using accounting expressions (like assets or net worth) to describe the problem, but that we are not looking at the problem, or the values, in accounting terms. We are looking at true values.

Fixed assets

In Example 7 in Chapter 8 we looked at an American company buying real estate in Italy for Lit800 million. Its problem was whether to borrow $1 million or Lit800 million to finance the purchase. The spot rate at the time was Lit800 = $1. In that example we assumed that we sold the property on the date of the next balance sheet, that in the meantime the lira/dollar exchange rate had moved, but that the lira price of the property had not changed. On these very special assumptions we found that the safest policy was to borrow lire; for on our assumptions the property constituted an asset at risk to a currency movement, so that it was safest to neutralize the risk by borrowing the currency of the asset.

That view is challenged by the *purchasing power parity theory*. This theory holds that in the long run exchange rates will adjust to divergent inflation rates in the countries concerned, so as to restore relative price levels in those countries to their starting-point. For example, if from the beginning of 1981 to the end of 1984 the inflation in Italy exceeded the inflation in the United States by 30% over the 4-year period, the theory would lead us to expect a decline in the lira against the dollar by that same 30%. If this were a reliable relationship, at least in the long run, then a truly risk-free policy for the long term would be to regard an Italian fixed asset as unexposed from the point of view of the dollar-based owner, and to finance its purchase by borrowing dollars.

Example 22   Purchasing power parity theory

On the above facts we assume that on 1 January 1981 Lit800 = $1. Between that date and 31 December 1983 we assume
(a) nil inflation in the United States, a total of 30% inflation in Italy
(b) nil inflation in Italy, and 30% inflation in the United States,
and we also assume that the inflation in one country is exactly matched by the depreciation of its currency against the other.

	(a)	(b)
Lire per dollar 1.1.81	800	800
Lire per dollar 31.12.83	1040	615
Lire value of property	Lit1040 million	Lit800 million
Dollar value of property	$1 000 000	$1 300 000
Dollar value of Lit800 million loan	$769 231	$1 300 000
Dollar value of dollar loan	$1 000 000	$1 000 000
Gain/(loss) from		
borrowing lire	$230 769	nil
borrowing dollars	nil	$300 000

At first sight, then, either policy can result in a gain, and neither in a loss! The explanation is that we have not taken into account the gain which anyone makes who borrows money during a period of inflation. In (b) we assume 30% inflation in the United States. A gain of $300 000 would have occurred in that case even if the property had been in the United States. Its value would have risen to $1 300 000, but the debt would have stayed put at $1 000 000. The $300 000 gain on borrowing dollars is explained by this fact, not by the currency movement. If we adjust for this inflation gain, the true currency effect compares as follows:

Gain/(loss) from		
borrowing lire	$230 769	($300 000)
borrowing dollars	nil	nil

Notes: (1) We do not have to adjust the figure in (a) for the inflation gain because we are comparing the outturn in dollars.

(2) The gain in (a) is $23.08\% = \dfrac{30}{130} \times 100$

The loss in (b) is $30\% = \dfrac{30}{100} \times 100$

(3) We are ignoring the effect of different interest rates. Chapter 22 deals with this. But we might expect rates to be higher where the inflation rate is higher. This would tend to reduce or eliminate the gain from inflation.

(4) The effects (if any) of tax are ignored.

The key assumption in Example 22 is that inflation in one country is exactly matched by the depreciation of its currency against the other, in which we assumed nil inflation. This is of course the contention of the purchasing power parity theory.

The theory as such is described and discussed by Aliber (1978). If we accept this theory, then we must ask ourselves how far we are willing to act on that acceptance. For example, are we willing to go so far as to declare that fixed assets are not part of our potential risk and should not therefore be financed with debt in local currency? This very point is discussed by Donaldson (1980, p. 96). He concludes that the risk of reduced real purchasing power is less than the risk of a reduction in the real capacity of the fixed assets to generate cash flow, that is, of its profitability not keeping up with inflation, so that the risk is commercial rather than financial. Consequently he considers that it 'may be acceptable to match out weak currency assets with weak currency liabilities', but not 'to match out a hard currency asset and in the process deliberately open up an unnecessary hard currency monetary liability'.

His first point is a helpful reminder of the nature of economic risk, which can be described in relation to an asset as a reduction due to a currency movement in the net present value of the future cash-flows which it can generate, expressed in the reporting currency.

It is probable that the best definition of the 'true' value of an asset would be in terms of the present value of the future net cash-flows which

112

it will generate. The practical difficulty is that the future net cash-flows are not actually known, and that any estimate of them may not demonstrably give us a better valuation than the current cost valuation. As the latter is more easily obtained, it is in practice a more convenient and not necessarily less accurate assessment of true value. In other words, we can accept the principle of Donaldson's criterion of value without departing from the practical advantage of using a current cost valuation.

But what about the proposition that the purchasing power parity theory would not support the borrowing of a strong currency to match or balance fixed assets held in that currency?

Example 23   Purchasing power parity and matching debt

An American company acquires a German process plant in year 1 for its open market value of DM3 million. Over the next 6 years there is a total of 100% inflation in the United States and 20% in Germany. On the date of purchase the spot rate was DM3 = $1. We assume that the purchasing power parity theory holds. The US company can finance the purchase by borrowing either DM3 million or $1 million.

	Purchase date	6 years later
Price level index, dollars	100	200
Price level index, D-marks	100	120
Spot rate DM per $	3.00	1.80
True DM value of plant	DM3 000 000	DM3 600 000
True $ value of plant	$1 000 000	$2 000 000
Dollar value of:		
DM borrowing	$1 000 000	$1 666 667
$ borrowing	$1 000 000	$1 000 000

The gearing gain from the borrowing therefore is $1 million (= $2 million value of plant less $1 million value of debt) if the company has borrowed dollars, but only $333 333 (i.e. $2 million − $1 666 667) if it has borrowed DM3 million instead of $1 million. The gain from borrowing dollars is equal to the whole of the inflationary doubling of the US price-level, whereas if the company had borrowed D-marks, the gain would have been reduced by the inflation differential of

$$\left(\frac{200}{120} - 1 \right) \$1 \text{ million} = \$666\ 667.$$

The example therefore shows a clear advantage in borrowing the weaker currency, which in this case is also the parent reporting currency, not the currency in which the asset is held. We must remember, however, that the advantage is likely to be reduced or eliminated by the probably higher interest cost of the currency with the higher inflation rate (the dollar), subject (as always) to the effect of tax.

However, the whole of both gains on the principal can be ascribed to the effect of gearing in conditions of inflation. The inflationary gain if the plant had been in the United States would have been $2 million − $1 million = $1 million. The gain if the company had been reporting in D-marks would have been DM3.6 million − DM3 million = DM600 000, which at DM1.80 = $1 comes to $333 333.

In fact, the example really only demonstrates that on our very special assumption of 100% correlation between currency movements and relative purchasing power we can, by borrowing the currency with the higher inflation rate, secure the greater inflation gain which that currency gives us.

The two Examples 22 and 23 show that if the exchange rate moves in exact proportion to the relative inflation rates, the true (defined as current cost for our purposes) value of fixed assets is not exposed to currency fluctuations, so that if we finance them by means of borrowings, the selection of the currency to borrow should not be made on currency risk management grounds. Indeed in these test-tube conditions a state of zero risk would be achieved by financing such fixed assets with parent company equity. The gains from gearing (subject to the effects of interest and tax) are the result of inflation, not of currency movements as such. In these conditions and on these assumptions it would therefore be reasonable to argue that if we borrow, we should restrict ourselves to weak currencies.

Objections to the view that fixed assets are not at risk

The objections to this view must rest on three broad categories of considerations:

1. Even if we are sure that our foreign fixed assets will maintain their true value in terms of our own currency, how do we know which currencies will be weak or strong to borrow?
2. The considerable reservations which we should have about the applicability of the purchasing power parity theory.
3. The intrinsic desirability of local currency borrowings as a protection against political risk, including the risk of exchange control restrictions and inconvertibility. This last point is of course peripheral to the topic of currency risk in the sense of risk from exchange rate movements.

Can we spot weak and strong currencies?

The first of these points is of considerable importance to the whole topic of currency risk management. That management would be relatively easy if we could always predict with confidence which currencies are strong or weak, that is, which will move up and which down. Looking back over the 1970s, we can probably see a long-term tendency for the D-mark and the Swiss franc to be strong and for the lira to be weak, but it would be much more difficult to be equally definite about the pound sterling, the French franc or the yen. In the early 1970s the Portuguese escudo was widely regarded as a strong currency; by the end of the decade it ranked among the weakest. Many currencies could have been classified as strong or weak by a glance at their average inflation rates, but what about sterling in 1976–80? At best we can say that *some* currency relationships have in the first decade of floating shown signs of being reliably classifiable. For example, a statement that the lira is normally weak against the Swiss franc would not very often be contradicted by experience. But even this could change, and the vast majority of exchange rates do not show nearly such a clear and consistent tendency. It is undeniable of course that there are many situations in which short-term movements can be confidently predicted to be either up or down, but when we talk about financing fixed assets, we are not concerned with short-term trends.

Reservations about purchasing power parity

The second broad cause for reservation was about the applicability of the purchasing power parity theory itself. Morgan Guaranty's measure of real effective exchange rates for 16 currencies from their March 1973 purchasing power showed that in December 1979, 6¾ years later, two (those of Sweden and France) were within 2½%, another five within 5% (those of the United States, Italy, Belgium, Netherlands and Denmark), a further four within 10% (Canada, Germany, Austria and Spain) of their March 1973 real values. The other five were Norway (down 11.1%), Switzerland (up 12.6%), Japan (down 13.1%), Australia (down 13.8%) and the United Kingdom (up 23.3%). Over these 6¾ years the record looks patchy. It is significant that seven currencies stayed within 5% and 11 within 10% of their original purchasing power parity, but the currencies which showed wider fluctuations include three major ones (Swiss franc, yen and sterling), and even fluctuations of 5 or 10% may well be enough to worry companies whose shareholders' funds are at risk. And of course, it is not much consolation for US companies, for example, that the dollar has not deviated from its purchasing power parity by more than about 5½%, if their fixed asset exposures are in Japan or Britain. The dollar/sterling rate, for example, has deviated wildly from its purchasing power parity.

But in any case, what validity the purchasing power parity relationship has tends to be a long-term one. The charts in Fig. 3 on pages 115–118 show that currencies deviate quite strongly from their purchasing

PRICE COMPETITIVENESS

- The charts below show the long-term movement of each country's relative prices expressed in $: the most recent picture is provided by the tables. Relative prices are calculated as the ratio of the 'dollar' prices in the country concerned to the weighted average of dollar prices in its trading partners, where the weights reflect the trading importance of each partner. The ratio is altered either by changes in the prices of goods and services (relative inflation) or by changes in the exchange rate.

- The ratio oscillates round clear long run trends. It is deviations from this trend which we use on the currency pages to provide an index of price competitiveness. The trends themselves in general do not represent changes in competitiveness. Rather they mostly reflect systematic differences in the price behaviour of domestic and of internationally traded goods because productivity in the two sectors is increasing at different rates.

- The last two observations are estimates, subject to significant revision.

US Dollar ($)

	Relative Wholesale Prices 1975=100	% Deviation from Trend
1979 1	94.6	−3.3
2	97.6	0.1
3	96.3	−0.8
4	99.0	2.3
1980 1	100.7	4.4
2	100.2	4.2
3	97.3	1.6
End Nov	102.3	7.2

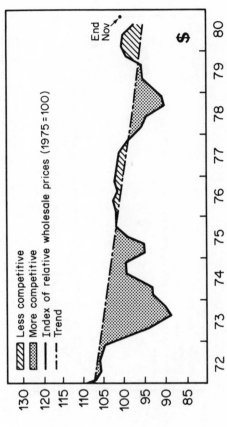

115

Pound Sterling (£)

	Relative Wholesale Prices 1975=100	% Deviation from Trend
1979 1	108.0	5.1
2	114.6	11.5
3	122.6	19.4
4	118.5	15.6
1980 1	125.6	22.5
2	129.0	26.0
3	133.0	30.0
End Nov	134.0	31.0

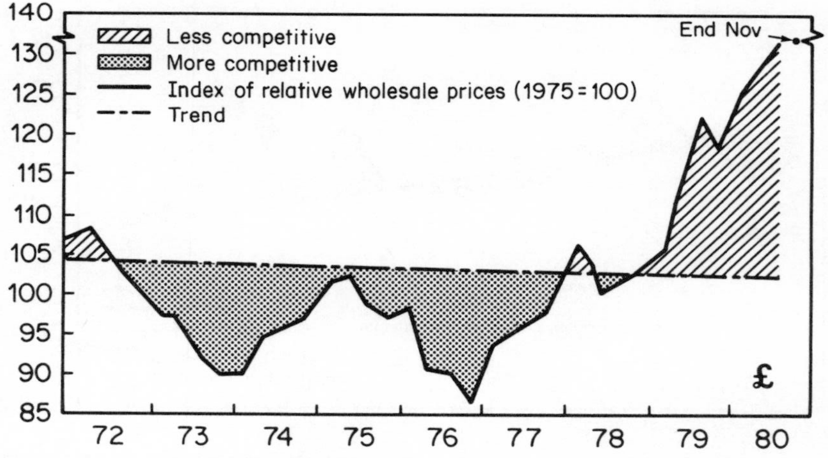
140
130
125
120
115
110
105
100
95
90
85
Less competitive
More competitive
Index of relative wholesale prices (1975=100)
Trend
End Nov
£
72
73
74
75
76
77
78
79
80

German Mark (DM)

	Relative Wholesale Prices 1975=100	% Deviation from Trend
1979 1	107.9	0.9
2	105.9	−1.3
3	106.4	−1.3
4	107.7	−0.6
1980 1	105.7	−2.9
2	102.2	−6.4
3	100.3	−8.5
End Nov	95.2	−13.6

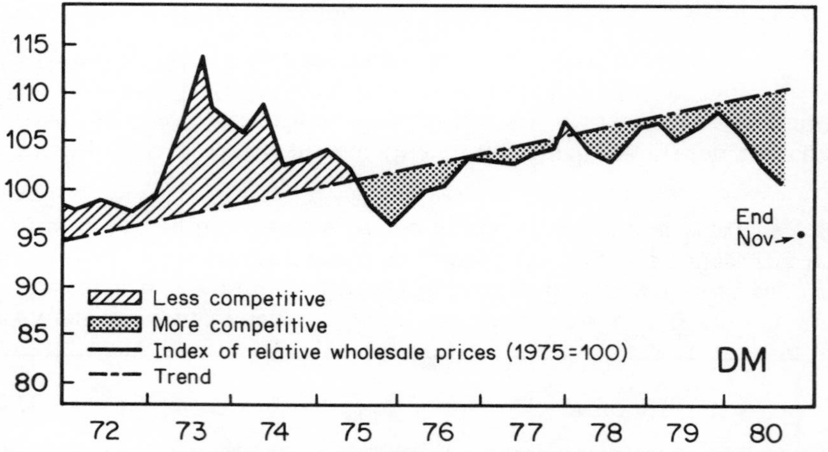
115
110
105
100
95
90
85
80
End Nov
Less competitive
More competitive
Index of relative wholesale prices (1975=100)
Trend
DM
72
73
74
75
76
77
78
79
80

117

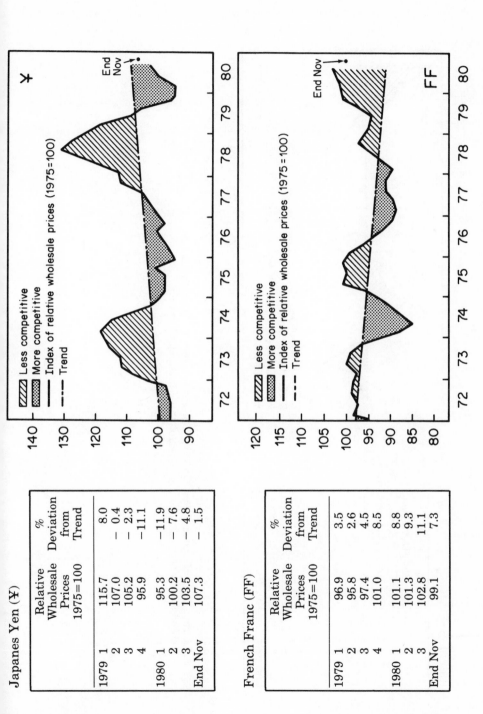

Japanes Yen (¥)

	Relative Wholesale Prices 1975=100	% Deviation from Trend
1979 1	115.7	8.0
2	107.0	− 0.4
3	105.2	− 2.3
4	95.9	−11.1
1980 1	95.3	−11.9
2	100.2	− 7.6
3	103.5	− 4.8
End Nov	107.3	− 1.5

French Franc (FF)

	Relative Wholesale Prices 1975=100	% Deviation from Trend
1979 1	96.9	3.5
2	95.8	2.6
3	97.4	4.5
4	101.0	8.5
1980 1	101.1	8.8
2	101.3	9.3
3	102.8	11.1
End Nov	99.1	7.3

Italian Lira (Lit)

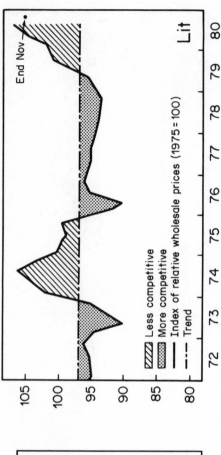

	Relative Wholesale Prices 1975=100	% Deviation from Trend
1979 1	94.4	3.4
2	96.9	−0.9
3	99.4	1.6
4	100.8	3.1
1980 1	101.6	3.9
2	104.6	7.0
3	106.3	8.7
End Nov	105.0	7.3

Fig. 3 Extract from *Exchange Rate Outlook*, December 1980, Charles Fulton. Reproduced by permission of Gower Publishing Company Limited.

power values in the short run, with strong movements both above and below that parity. And to cap it all, those same charts tend to show that most currencies have a long-term trend which moves their real parities either up or down. The trend lines are downward for the dollar, sterling, French franc and lira, and strongly upward for the D-mark and yen. Economists explain this long-term tendency.for purchasing power parities to slope up or down as caused by differences in relative productivity in the various countries, and the effects of those differences on goods and services which are not widely traded across frontiers (like local newspapers, local rail fares, haircuts and restaurant meals). This long-term trend in purchasing power parity tends to cut the ground from under the feet of those who wish to rely on purchasing power theory as a foundation of their currency risk management policies.

We must remember again that we are not in this chapter concerned with any corporate objective which measures currency risk in terms of accounting effects. We are concerned with the risk, if any, which flows from the 'true' value of fixed assets, and we have for practical purposes identified that value as equal to current cost. In these terms, the most serious problem thrown up in these doubts about the validity of the purchasing power theory is that it quite evidently does not apply in the short run. We can, for instance, observe long periods when exchange rates are largely influenced by relative interest rates, which can vary substantially from relative inflation rates for such periods. And directors of companies may well be reluctant to leave their companies unprotected against short-term fluctuations in the currencies in which they have true imbalances due to the location of fixed assets in the areas of those currencies. For example, a liquidity crisis can come to a company at relatively short notice, and directors might then wish to be free to realize assets without having to worry whether such disposals would realize substantial currency losses.

The third and last category of objections to the view that fixed assets held in a non-parent currency should not be financed with local currency debt, was that local borrowings can be an important defence against *political* risk. Political risk is discussed in detail in Chapter 24. The concept embraces not only the risk of expropriation or being put out of business by war or other political disturbance, but also the risk of exchange controls, penal withholding taxes, and any other legal or fiscal obstacles to the repatriation of earnings, intercompany loans, or equity capital invested.

Conclusion about fixed assets

To sum up, the view that fixed assets should not be financed by debt in the same currency, or at least not if that currency is a strong one, can be defended only if all the following conditions are fulfilled:

1. We have sound reason to believe that the currency is and will remain consistently strong, that is, will rise against the reporting currency.
2. We are either not concerned to avoid a balance sheet risk on the currency in the short term, or convinced that the purchasing power theory holds in the short as well as the long term.
3. We do not believe that the currency has a long-term tendency to fall against its purchasing power parity with our reporting currency.
4. We have no cause for concern about the political risk in the country where the assets are located.

We may well take the view that these conditions will only in very rare cases all be fulfilled.

Inventories

Inventories have given rise to separate discussions of exchange risk mainly because they are strictly a historically valued asset when valued at cost, and therefore one of those assets which the temporal method requires companies to translate at the historical rate of exchange. In this chapter we are not concerned with accounting risks, but with true risks. We can, however, safely say that inventories are a very minor problem in both accounting and true terms. This is because we could without much compunction describe them as a near-current value item. Obviously, when they are valued at net realizable values, they are currently valued items anyway.

One reason why fixed assets are such a troublesome item is that their historical values can be many years out of date, and therefore give rise to major differences in terms of the local currency. This problem seldom arises with inventories which are for the most part of low age and therefore valued at near current values. Their true value may well be their current cost, which is after all defined as their up-to-date value to the business. For practical purposes there should be no difference between the accounting concept of current cost and the non-accounting concept of true value which at present concerns us. And even if we compare historical values of inventories with current values, we should not expect to find differences as spectacular as are found with fixed assets.

For our purposes, then, we classify inventories as a short-term problem, and therefore in the same risk category as monetary items, with which we deal next.

Monetary assets and liabilities

Eyebrows might well be raised at the very thought that we need to discuss whether monetary items are part of the true currency risk. If items are determined in money values, there can be no argument on grounds of purchasing power parity. So what is the problem?

The problem comes from the Fisher Open theorem, which asserts that differences between interest rates on similar assets denominated in different currencies will adjust to the expected rate of change in the exchange rates between the currencies concerned.

Anyone who has kept graphs of forward rates (which fairly faithfully reproduce the difference between Eurocurrency interest rates), and the actual spot rates on the forward dates, knows that this equation is a far from accurate prediction of future spot rates. Indeed, if both the purchasing power parity and Fisher Open relationships were reliable and continuously reliable, then

> regardless of the currency mix of the firm's assets and liabilities, its income, its net worth, and presumably its market value would not be affected by changes in the exchange rates. The firm would not be subject to risk if the realized returns could not differ from the expected returns. These propositions provide a useful benchmark for assessment of risk; however, if they fully described the financial world, books on exchange risk would soon be redundant. (Aliber, 1978, p. 135.)

Any idea that the Fisher Open theorem would in practice, even if it were continuously valid, leave companies indifferent to currency risk on monetary assets and liabilities, would of course also have to be modified by considerations of taxation and accounting. Interest is in most circumstances an item which attracts tax if earned, and is deductible for tax if paid. It is also practically always a revenue item in the profit and loss account. Any profit or loss on the principal amount of a monetary asset or liability, on the other hand, can have a great variety of effects on the company's liability to tax, ranging from nil to full taxation at the company's rate of tax on income, and stopping in the middle at a point where the effect is at the rate on capital gains. In many cases the treatment is asymmetrical, in that gains are taxed but losses are not allowed as a deduction. Similarly, gains and losses on the principal amount of a monetary item are in many accounting standards treated as changes in a reserve and in others as ordinary income or expenditure.

Few companies could ignore these technical factors even if they believed that after allowing for changes in net interest income or expense the effect of currency movements would be neutral.

All treasurers act on the assumption that monetary assets and liabilities are at least a part of the risk which they have to manage, and the conclusion must be that on all counts they are correct in that belief.

Conclusions

In this chapter we have examined whether fixed assets, or inventories, or monetary assets and liabilities, are outside the items which contribute to 'true' balance sheet risk. We have found that all of them are part of that risk, and that for practical purposes the quantification of true risk should take all of them into account *at current values*. This is not because current values are or might become a general accounting convention, but because true risk is best ascertained and measured at current values.

In the next chapter we look at whether our definitions of balance sheet and trading risk give rise to any gaps or overlaps between them.

References

Aliber, R. Z. (1978). *Exchange Risk and Corporate International Finance*, Macmillan, London, pp. 26–29 and 106.

Donaldson, J. A. (1980). *Corporate Currency Risk*, The Financial Times Business Information Ltd., London.

CHAPTER 19

The Borderline Between Trading Risk and Balance Sheet Risk

Trade receivables and payables

When we examined the netting matrix method of managing trading risks in Chapter 14, we found that the netting matrix is in its very essence a way of managing exposures as balance sheet risks rather than trading risks. In the field of balance sheet risk we have one exposure for each maturity in each currency, whereas in the field of trading risk we have one exposure for each maturity for each pricing decision. Trading exposure is a much more fragmented concept, and it ceases to be managed as a trading exposure when it is no longer managed against the exchange rate used in the original pricing decision.

This question can be raised in a more general form. Trading risk begins with the pricing decision where the currency of the price is not the currency of cost, and it is likely to end on the balance sheet as (say) a receivable or a payable. If we then manage the balance sheet risk, do we have to exclude the receivables and payables because they are being managed as trading risk? If we include them in the calculation of our balance sheet risk, are we managing the same risk twice? Or are we in danger of undoing the good we have done with our trading risk management? In other words, do the two concepts overlap?

The answer turns out to be that there is no such conflict or overlap as long as we adopt the correct treatment of trading items which we have covered forward.

If a company in Italy has dollar receivables which it has sold forward for lire, those receivables are fixed in terms of lire, not dollars, and must not be counted as part of the dollar exposure on the balance sheet. If the receivables have not been sold forward, then they do count as part of the dollar risk. If the receivables have been sold forward for D-marks because the costs are in D-marks, then they count as part of the Italian company's D-mark assets, for the purpose of determining its balance sheet risk in D-marks.

If on the other hand the Italian company has hedged its trading risk on dollar receivables by borrowing dollars, then of course both the dollar

123

receivables and the dollar liability on the debt count as part of the dollar balance sheet risk, but will cancel out if we have built our hedge correctly.

There is, therefore, no danger of double hedging action, as long as we classify our receivables and payables correctly. Our Italian company should only treat those dollar receivables as part of its dollar position, which it has not sold forward for lire. By definition, these receivables are exposures which it has not already hedged and which it can now legitimately hedge as part of its action to neutralize its balance sheet risk.

(It might of course reasonably be asked why an Italian company should *wish* to hedge its dollar receivables, as many people feel there is ample evidence that the dollar is normally strong against the lira, but we should remember that our general approach in this book is to describe currency risk management in terms which aim at zero risk and then to envisage controlled departures from zero in precisely this kind of case. We have to establish the normal principles before we can depart from them.)

It is instructive at this stage to trace the career of a particular trading exposure. During its early stages we can manage it as a trading risk, that is, with the aim of doing at least no worse than the rate of exchange used in the pricing decision. At some perhaps much later stage it may be unrealistic to look back to the original pricing decision. When this is the case, it is more economical (in terms of management effort, currency dealing costs, and perhaps data processing resources) to treat it as part of the balance sheet risk. And we have already noted that there is a close kinship between the netting matrix method and the general technique of managing balance sheet risk, because there is only one risk for each maturity in each currency.

It is of course very important to remember that a trading risk does not cease to be a trading risk in terms of its tax effect or (at least under some accounting conventions) its accounting effects. What we are here saying is simply that the concept of trading risk is inseparable from the pricing decision, and that if we fail to hedge a risk in its early stages, there will come a time when we can no longer sensibly *manage* it against the pricing decision, and that from that point onwards the correct attitude towards it is to see it as part of the task of *managing* the balance sheet risk. This is simply because we can then forget all the individual pricing decisions.

What is the point at which this important change occurs? The easiest answer is the circular one: at whatever point the exchange rate which went into the pricing decision ceases to be relevant as a management criterion. But why does it cease to be relevant? In some companies it never *was* relevant, because they neglect the currency aspect of the pricing decision and fail to give enough weight to that aspect and its professional problems. In some cases, especially where the exposure only takes 3 or 4 months from the pricing decision to the collection of cash, the profit effect is overshadowed by any gain or loss already taken if an annual accounting date has occurred between those two dates. But the most important reason must be that there comes a point at which there is no longer any rationale for managing against the rate in the pricing decision. Either the spot rate and the available forward rate to maturity of the risk are by then so unfavourable that it would be more rational to cut our loss and ensure that we do not make it any larger, or the rate is so much better than the pricing rate that we should no longer be content to achieve that rate. There comes a point where bygones are bygones, or (to use an even more relevant cliché) where the horse is too far down the road to justify us in locking the stable door. We could try to press this logic one step further. Why should it make sense at such a late stage for us to start paying attention to the exchange rate which went into the pricing decision, if we have not concerned ourselves with it up to the point of birth of the exposure, that is, the point at which we are either commercially or contractually committed to the trading transaction?

Without getting dogmatic about it, we are therefore reaching the conclusion that trading risk should cease to be managed as trading risk and begin to be managed as part of the balance sheet risk as soon as it is postnatal. Many people will shake their heads and regard this as rather early in the life of the exposure, but others will think it rather late. *Their* argument will probably centre around the antenatal risk in the tender period for a large contract or project. Once we have made our pricing decision for the tender (they will argue), what can we do about it? How can we go on managing the exposure against the pricing decision after our tender has been submitted?

The answer to that is threefold. First, not all trading risks involve an antenatal stage. Some prices are negotiated at the same time as the order is accepted and placed, and in those cases the pricing rate may well cease to have management significance as soon as we take the decision not to cover forward at that same time. Secondly, when we submit large tenders, the currency risk management action at that point in time should involve two elements: (a) the determination of the worst rate at which we might reasonably expect to sell the contract receipts forward if the contract were awarded to us at the end of the validity period of the tender price, and at that price; and (b) the decision to sell the receipts forward in that event. In other words, the management process would involve two stages, the last at the point of birth of the exposure. Thirdly, and most importantly, tenders are rarely quite simply awarded within their validity period. If they are, then under English law, for example, our offer has been accepted, and our tender price has become contractually binding. But if this occurs after the end of the validity period, or if the customer wishes to negotiate different or more detailed terms than those specified in the tender, then his award of the contract is only a counter-offer, and we are legally and contractually free to review our currency price. This may of course be commercially imprudent or unattractive, but the company would be unwise to relax its attention to the currency risk while there is still any chance of renegotiating an exchange conversion rate which has turned out catastrophic as a result of unexpected adverse movements in the currency market. To sum up, there are very strong arguments against any suggestion that the pricing rate can cease to be the subject of risk management before the risk itself has passed the point of birth and become postnatal.

Our conclusion, therefore, is that trading risk continues to be trading risk for management purposes until birth, and that thereafter it is normally best managed as part of the balance sheet risk in the currency concerned, provided of course that we remember that its tax and accounting characteristics remain those of a trading transaction. But it is no use pretending that this conclusion is not a startling one.

What is startling about this, is that many companies, among them some with prestigious currency management teams, do not manage trading exposures until after the stage of birth, but nevertheless speak of balance sheet risk as something quite different. And here we are saying that after the stage of birth there is only one kind of currency risk management problem, that of balance sheet risks.

We can of course distinguish many different kinds of problems within the balance sheet risk field. Risks which began as trading risks retain their tax and accounting characteristics. These risks also tend to originate in the commercial or marketing area, whereas balance sheet risk outside that field of trade receivables and payables tends to be more amenable to purely financial management. But a much more relevant distinction is that between monetary items and non-monetary items. This also broadly corresponds with the distinction between those which have and those which do not have definite maturity dates. If three months from now a non-German company has more D-mark receipts than payments maturing, it should make a decision whether to hedge that excess by forward cover or borrowing D-marks, or to leave the exposure uncovered. But (tax apart) does it make any difference whether the items are in respect of trade purchases or sales, or capital purchases or disposals, or loan maturities, rental instalments, or dividends, or royalties? It is surely hard to see why it should make any difference. On the other hand non-monetary items do cause different problems, as we saw in the last chapter. There are reasonable grounds for at least enquiring whether they cause risk at all, and there is a difficulty about ascribing a duration or maturity to a non-monetary exposure, for no hedging action can be accurately aimed at an unspecified maturity date.

Dividends, royalties, management charges, etc.

In Chapter 17 we looked at outstanding intercompany dividends, royalties, interest or management charges within a group of companies. When they are undischarged balances, they represent an opportunity to accelerate or delay payment, and they nearly always involve an opportunity to cover forward or not. Each such decision affects the group balance in each currency and is therefore a balance sheet risk management decision. Within a group they do not normally involve any external pricing decision; hence in our terms they do not involve trading risk management as long as they relate to intragroup transactions. Items like royalties, interest and other charges do of course frequently occur between unrelated parties across frontiers, in which case pricing decisions can arise. But this is rare. Dividends normally have to be denominated in the currency in which profits are ascertained. Interest has to be charged in the currency of the loan. Royalties are occasionally quantified in a currency other than that in which the sales are denominated, and management charges can be levied in either currency, that of the company which gives or the one which receives the management service. But even where there are such decisions, they tend to occur on the rare occasion when a royalty or management agreement is under negotiation. On those rare occasions they should be managed as trading risks, but this is a tiny exception to the general rule that all these items give rise to the problems of balance sheet risk management. That is where we have to classify the overwhelming majority of these risks.

Capital expenditure purchases

These clearly belong to the same category as trading transactions. Every purchase decision for a fixed asset must involve a pricing decision. In fact we have grandiose names for some of these processes, like investment appraisal or evaluation. In each such case a purchase in a currency other than our normal reporting or operating currency must involve an explicit or implicit exchange rate assumption, and that pricing decision must be managed up to the point of commitment. Currency expertise should go into the exchange rate assumption. If the source of the purchase is not economic at an exchange rate which currency expertise tells us is attainable, then alternative sources or assets should be considered and compared. And when the buying decision has been made, the cash payments should be hedged by one of the available hedging devices so as to ensure that the economics of the purchase are not invalidated by an adverse currency movement. This is the moment of birth. If we have not then hedged it, the item becomes a balance sheet risk, or rather part of our total net exposure in the currency concerned.

Postnatal items not yet on the balance sheet

All the items which we have discussed in this chapter, trade payables and receivables, capital expenditure payables and royalties, dividends, management and interest charges, are quite capable of being postnatal commitments before they would feature on a balance sheet. This is because under normal accounting principles assets, and the amounts owed for their purchase, are not entered in the accounting records until the title has passed to the reporting company.

This distinction does not, however, concern us in currency risk management. We have a postnatal risk as soon as we have a contractual or commercial commitment, and this has nothing to do with the passing of title. We must, therefore, be careful to define our balance sheet risks so as to include these postnatal items which are not yet visible on a balance sheet.

CHAPTER 20

Other Problems in Defining True Balance Sheet Risk

Valuation of true balance sheet risk

We have effectively already dealt with all the valuation problems in Chapter 18. We saw that all monetary items should of course be taken at their face values, fixed assets at current values and inventories also at current values which are not likely to be substantially different in most cases from the values at which they stand in the balance sheet even in terms of historical cost accounts. In Example 24 in Chapter 21 we shall see a good illustration of how such a true valuation differs from an accounting valuation.

Moreover, we are concerned with the risk in any one currency other than the reporting currency of the company or group. So these valuation principles must be applied to all assets and liabilities on the balance sheet, plus postnatal trading commitments not yet on the balance sheet, and denominated in the currency. But all items which have been covered forward, count as part of the exposure in the currency for which they have been bought or sold forward, not the currency in which they are denominated.

When does balance sheet risk begin?

Here above all we need a theory which fits reality as we find it. Reality seems to consist of three types of risk for this purpose:

* Some risks originate from time to time through investment decisions, such as acquisition, capital expenditure or expansion projects. They should be managed *at birth*. If our corporate posture is defensive, we can for example finance them by debt in matching currencies.
* Other significant risks can arise from financing decisions, if we deliberately accept liabilities which exceed group assets in a particular currency. We should not normally do this at all unless we

have an aggressive corporate policy on risk management and under this deliberately borrow a currency which we believe to be reliably weaker than the currencies of the assets financed with this debt.

* But most risks turn up when we analyse our consolidated position either for the first time, or for the first time after a period in which that position has undergone significant currency changes, perhaps organically in the course of ordinary trading. If such a scrutiny reveals a large imbalance in a currency, the only sensible way to look at it is as a risk which begins at the time that we recognize and identify it. In reality it obviously started before that, but that earlier biography has no management significance. Bygones cannot concern us. Strictly, we should also regard each fluctuation up or down in this risk as the birth or death of an individual mini-risk, but in practice no company can afford to fragment its risk management effort to that extent.

Our general answer therefore is that the true balance sheet risk in each currency begins when we identify it, but that all significant investment and financing decisions should be managed at birth. We have already taken the view that in practice there will hardly be any antenatal balance sheet risks. In the normal course of events projects do not become commitments before companies can take the corresponding financing decisions.

Against what base exchange rate do we measure the risk?

This question is so closely related to the previous one that the answers follow from those we have just given. If the risk is a new one, and the result of a new investment or financing decision, then our risk is that of doing worse than the rate used in that decision. If on the other hand the risk is a newly perceived imbalance in a particular currency, then the rate must be the one ruling at the time that we first perceive it. For instance, if at 2.30 pm on 7 April we look at a printout of the balance sheet position (adjusted so as to show us the true risk) at 31 March, then we are concerned not with the rate on 31 March, but with the rate at 2.30 pm on 7 April at which we could take hedging action if we so wished.

When does the risk end?

This is a more difficult question. Strictly, we are concerned not with the actual duration, observed with hindsight, but with the *expected* duration for which we should manage the risk.

Balance sheet risk affects each company, and also the group; and this distinction applies not just to the accounting concept of risk. Within each company all the monetary items will tend to have definite maturity dates, and even where a current account balance in a contract may mature on some unknown date on which a milestone in the performance of the contract has been reached, we can usually estimate the due date within a matter of weeks or months rather than years. More difficult are overdrafts or other short-term borrowings which we know can in practice be extended or rolled over. They should nevertheless be regarded as repayable within one year or (where this is more appropriate) at their legal maturity.

Most complex is the question of non-monetary items. Once again inventories are not the main problem. They are usually destined to be turned into cash at times which can be estimated within reasonable limits. But *fixed assets* are not normally held with the object of realization for cash. At one extreme end there is land which theoretically has an infinite life; at the other end we may have some short-life assets which are too valuable to be written off to revenue. As we are concerned with true risk, not accounting risk, we have to make realistic assessments in broad categories spanning (say) 2½, 5, 10, 15, 20, 25 and 30 years. In estimating their business lives we should of course think in product and market terms and assume that no asset, not even land, has an indefinite life in any one business use. All this presupposes that we regard fixed assets as part of our exposure, notwithstanding the purchasing power parity theory which we looked at in Chapter 18.

So much for the maturity problem in the single company. When we come to consider the balance sheet risk of a group of companies, we must have a look at the island theory or net investment approach. In Chapter 8 we saw that both the FASB and the British Accounting Standards Committee in their exposure drafts of autumn 1980 adopted this approach for the purpose of translation accounting. In this chapter we are not concerned with accounting, but the island theory is an important concept which transcends the accounting issues and has great significance for our perception of true risk.

The island theory or net investment approach

When we have a major expansion project or a project to acquire a new subsidary, this usually involves adding the whole gamut of fresh net operating asset categories to our balance sheet. There are likely to be fixed assets, inventories, receivables and payables. We can look at the whole of this future collection of assets and liabilities in a fragmented way, in which case we shall no doubt look at the receivables and payables as items with short maturities. Or we can look at the entire project as a unit which we are adding as a single long-term entity to our group position. There will be some 30-day receivables in the new subsidiary, but if we look at the subsidiary at annual or even 5-year intervals into the future, we automatically think of these as revolving, in other words, as perpetually self-renewing as each month's sales produce fresh receivables to replace those which we collect and turn into cash.

Each of these perceptions, one fragmented and one monolithic, sheds light on the nature of the project and each teaches us something. J A Donaldson (1980) has described the currency implications of the monolithic approach, which he calls the island theory, in his recent article.

At this moment we are concerned with maturities of balance sheet risks. If we take the fragmented view, then the 30-day receivables of the new subsidiary are short-term risks; if we take the island (or monolithic) view, then they are long-term risks, and in that case the whole expansion project or acquisition project has to be allocated an estimated duration, presumably a long one of several decades in most cases. We had so far only looked at this as a problem concerning fixed assets.

It is probable that most companies will in most cases regard the monolithic or island view as more realistic, especially at the point of origin of the acquisition project. Its validity, moreover, is likely to be least challenged in this context of maturity of balance sheet risk. It makes sense to look at a whole subsidiary as a long-term investment by the group.

Reservations about the island theory

There are however two reservations which must be made about the island concept, one about its applicability to certain situations and one about its quantification.

The first point is that there will be cases in which the parts are more significant than the whole, where the individual assets and liabilities will concern us more than the operation or subsidiary as such. An example is a company which is in the construction or engineering contracting field, and whose activity at any given time is heavily concentrated in a few, perhaps a dozen or two contracts, and whose operating capital is employed in working capital rather than fixed assets. In such a case the acquiring company may well regard itself as investing in the larger contracts rather than in the business as a whole, as there is no way of forecasting what the pattern of future contracts will be, in terms of individual size, location, or currencies. It would be difficult to look upon such a subsidiary as a long-term exposure in Swedish kronor if the contracts may well turn up in Saudi Arabian riyals, US dollars or yen. This is only one illustration of a case where the parts may well concern us more than the whole.

The other point is that we cannot ignore the parts where significant assets or liabilities are not in the reporting (or functional) currency of the subsidiary. If the company permanently exports all its output in a currency which is neither its own nor that of the parent company, and carries the receivables unhedged, then it has a significant asset which is not from the parent company's point of view an exposure in the local currency of the subsidiary. The same would be true if the subsidiary had a large third-currency debt among its liabilities. A very simple example, with all items valued at current price or cost levels would be this one:

Example 24

The UK parent has an Italian subsidiary with the following position in current lira values (all items in millions of lire)

Shareholders funds	2500	US dollar receivables	1700
Yen bond	1200	Lira assets less liabilities	2000
	3700		3700

The net investment or island approach in this case is valid, but the net lira investment of the parent company is not Lit2500 million, but Lit2500 million + Lit1200 million − Lit1700 million = Lit2000 million. The yen bond is not a negative *lira* exposure, and the dollar receivables are not a positive one.

Our conclusions about the maturities or duration of balance sheet risk, therefore, are that within each company we have to assess maturities in a manner appropriate to each class of asset, but that for the group as a whole we must modify that approach to the extent that the island or net investment approach applies to whole subsidiaries or operations, and in so far as those subsidiaries have their assets and liabilities in their local currencies.

In which currency is balance sheet risk measured?

When we tackled trading risks, we concluded that where neither costs nor price were in the reporting currency, it was best not to define or manage risk in that currency. In the field of balance sheet risk we are concerned with net total balances in each currency. Consequently we need a clear standard against which we measure gains, losses and risks. As in most other questions about balance sheet risk, we must distinguish between risk in one company and risk to the group.

It seems clear that in most cases the currency of measurement will be the currency in which the company or group reports its results and financial position. This may well be due to the coincidence that the great majority of companies present their financial statements in the currency in which they operate, in which their capital is denominated, and in which they have to measure their legal position, and particularly their solvency. But this convenient correspondence is by no means universal. Many US-controlled companies find it convenient to keep their accounts in US dollars, and will prepare local currency accounts only if obliged by local law to file such accounts. Wherever the reporting currency is not the local currency, companies would do well to remember that a local insolvency could have costly and burdensome consequences for the whole group of companies. There is much to be said for measuring currency risk for each company in that currency in which their legal solvency is measured in their local jurisdiction.

In purely financial terms, alternative views are possible. As a case in point, a Brazilian company with more cruzeiro assets than liabilities might not be content to avoid currency loss in terms of cruzeiros. It might well adopt a corporate objective to maintain or increase its net worth in terms of US dollars.

Again, there is the case of a large financial institution in the United Kingdom or Italy, competing with rivals in Germany, Switzerland and France. Such an institution might well feel that its main competitive weapon is the size of its net worth relative to that of its competitors. It might, therefore, wish to measure its currency risk in terms of either a strong currency like the D-mark or in terms of a basket of currencies like the European Unit of Account or the SDR. Another case is that of the true multinational like Shell or Unilever, which has its financial ownership based in more than one country. It too might not be content to measure its currency position in just one currency.

But for our present purposes it is enough to draw attention to these important exceptions, and to use the convenient expression 'reporting currency' to denote the currency in which a company wishes to measure its currency risk.

What goes for the individual company, must go for the group too. Each parent company of a group will have its measuring currency which we, to avoid being pedantic, call its reporting currency, and this is bound to differ from the reporting currency of at least some of its foreign subsidiaries. The ideal defensive practice is for each company to balance its own position in the currencies in which it should not be exposed, and for the parent company to ensure that the group position is balanced out, mainly by adjusting the currency portfolio of its own balance sheet. In many cases a group may have good reasons, especially reasons prompted by exchange control regulations or tax rules, for arranging equal and opposite imbalances in different group companies, but it will have to do this within the constraints of the need to keep each individual subsidiary solvent and compliant with its local legal obligations.

It is important for the parent company to watch and manage the overall balance in each currency of the group as a whole, but contrary to the view expressed by some writers a group may easily find itself with good reasons for reducing its position in a certain currency in one subsidiary and for increasing it elsewhere. The fact that most subsidiaries have to measure their currency risk in their own local currencies helps to explain this.

Final definition of true balance sheet risk

The next chapter deals with those aspects of currency risk which arise from accounting treatment. In the last three chapters we have completed our review of the nature of balance sheet risk as seen by a board which was not concerned with the accounting effect of its actions, but was anxious to define and control its true exposure to that risk in the balance sheet field. We can now define true balance sheet risk as follows:

It is the risk to a company or a group of companies which has an imbalance between exposed assets and liabilities in any currency other than its reporting currency, of a loss to its true net worth from any adverse movement between that currency and the reporting currency from the exchange rate at which that imbalance was first accepted or perceived. There is one such risk for each currency in which there is an imbalance, and for management purposes each such risk needs to be subdivided by maturity periods. In assessing maturity periods for a group, it is necessary for the group to define whether it regards each subsidiary as a single long-term investment or as a collection of assets and liabilities with different maturities. In this definition 'exposed' assets or liabilities include those bought or sold forward for the currency concerned, but not those originally denominated in it and sold or bought forward for another currency; they are now part of the exposure in that latter currency. 'Exposed' assets and liabilities also include postnatal trading or similar commitments which are not yet visible on a balance sheet drawn up for accounting purposes. As we are concerned here with true, as distinct from accounting, risk, exposed assets are valued at their true values to the business, which for practical purposes can be equated with current values.

It is important to remember that this definition applies to true risk only. Companies are often concerned with currency risk as it affects their published financial figures, and the next chapter deals with the implications of that view of balance sheet risk.

For the moment, however, we need to stress only one point. We have in these last three chapters used the expression 'true' balance sheet risk rather than 'transaction' risk, because we saw in Chapter 6 that the distinction between transaction and accounting risk is purely a question of whether the risk manager is concerned with the whole of the life of the risk or only that part which ends at the next accounting date. In that sense true risk evidently includes the concept of transaction risk. The distinction between true and accounting risk, however, covers a wider set of issues, such as whether certain classes of assets form part of the risk and how assets must be valued in order to quantify the risk correctly. The expression 'transaction' risk remains useful because it shows us a feature which trading and balance sheet risk have in common, but it cannot be used as a synonym for true risk.

Reference

Donaldson, J. A. (1980), 'Managing Currency Exposures after the end of exchange controls', *The Banker*, **August**.

CHAPTER 21

Should we Manage the Accounting Risk Rather than the True Balance Sheet Risk?

What difference would it make?

Before we turn to the choice between managing true and accounting risk in this balance sheet area, we must get a clear idea of what the difference is.

For this purpose we must have a look at the following topics:

* which assets and liabilities are included in the risk,
* valuation of risks,
* neutralizing risk in a single company,
* the distinction between a group and its member companies,
* the time-horizon of risk management.

Assuming current value accounting

Cutting across these topics are the two questions of which set of accounting conventions concern us, and whether we are translating historical cost accounts or accounts drawn up at current, i.e. inflation-adjusted values.

We immediately find that in practice this last point wraps up all our valuation problems. In Chapter 18 we decided that for practical purposes we can equate 'true' with current value, so that current value accounts show assets at what we are here calling their 'true' value. This applies even to the temporal method, which requires assets and liabilities carried at current values to be translated at the closing exchange rate. This removes the biggest conflict between the temporal and other translation conventions.

In any case we had concluded in Chapter 18 that, except in some very rare conditions, fixed assets and other non-monetary items had to be regarded as being exposed to 'true' currency risk. Again therefore on this topic there is no conflict between managing accounting and true risk: in both cases we have to manage the whole of the net position in each currency.

Now how about the problem of neutralizing risk in a single company? It is the same story. As long as the closing rate method is used, we ensure that the assets are translated at the same rate as the debt with which we finance them. Conflict would therefore arise only if the standard for translation is the temporal method. Under ED 21 and ED 27 the closing rate is the norm anyhow. So again there is no problem under any translation standard, as long as the basic accounting is at current values. In these conditions, if we adjust the debt in each currency so as to bring assets and liabilities into balance, currency gains and losses will occur neither in true nor in accounting terms.

Treatment of all gains and losses in one company as part of ordinary profit or loss before taxation

What could, however, cause us to perceive a potential conflict even if the accounts are current value accounts, is the reluctance of all the standards under review except ED 21 to allow any currency differences in a single company to be treated other than as an ordinary trading gain or loss, unless Appendix 5 of ED 27 gives some limited relief from this rule. There could be cases in which we might not perceive the accounting result as portraying the true nature of the currency gains and losses. This may particularly be the case where a currency rate tends to fluctuate up and down with no clear long-term trend, so that the gains and losses do not carry conviction as being akin to cash flow changes. This is a real case of potential conflict, but it is not likely to be significant or substantial in any company or group where the attitude to currency risk is defensive, and where this risk-averse attitude is adopted in each company and not just for the group as a whole. In other words, this problem is likely to have practical consequences mainly where companies pursue more aggressive risk management policies or where defensive policies are pursued for the group rather than for each company, in the reasonable desire to save dealing and administrative costs.

The group versus each company in it

We next come to the distinction between the group and all its members. ED 21 and FAS 8 did not emphasize the distinction, but ED 27 and its US counterpart do. Under them any company, including the parent company, which records a translation gain or loss, must treat this as part of the ordinary results before tax, and this treatment cannot be undone in the group consolidation. It is therefore these exposure drafts which give rise to potential conflict.

The restrictions which the 1980 exposure drafts place on the cover method are the main problem. Even if ED 27 were ultimately liberalized to extend the cover method to gains and losses on loans of a holding company used to finance net investments, for the purposes of its own accounts, there is still the heavy constraint that it must be the holding company (and not for instance a fellow subsidiary) that has to be the borrower, and that the offset is restricted to the gain or loss on the net worth of the subsidiary (plus long-term loans from the holding company), even where the exposure is much greater because the subsidiary has non-local currency debt.

But we must not exaggerate the practical effect of these restrictions. Many groups will think twice before leaving unhedged positions in those subsidiaries which are partly owned or thinly capitalized. The interests of outside shareholders have to be protected, and that protection is not achieved by equal and opposite positions elsewhere in the group. And where the net worth of a company is small, an unhedged risk can jeopardize its legal solvency and ability to trade. And again, where the group position is in balance but there are imbalances in some currencies in some companies, some of the losses which go through the profit and loss account to the consolidated results before tax, will at that point be netted out against some of the gains made in the rest of the group (since they are not the kind of gains which have to be dealt with in the reserves because they arise only on consolidation).

Nevertheless, many groups may be forced to incur unnecessary costs in balancing their positions in each and every group company as a consequence of these new accounting conventions.

Maturity of risks

Continuing still with our assumption that the separate accounts of the group companies are at current and not historic values, we look finally at the time-span for which we manage currency risk. We have already looked at this in Chapter 6. We can either manage each risk for its entire known or estimated duration: in that case we are managing it as transaction risk which is part and parcel of our concept of true risk. Or we can manage it for the period up to the next accounting date; in that case we are managing it as accounting risk. We saw in Chapter 6 that so long as our aim is to manage defensively, this choice need not cause a dilemma. For when we manage a risk for its entire life-span, we automatically also neutralize it for the intervening accounting dates. The two 1980 exposure drafts confirm that this will be the effect in the accounts at those intermediate dates. The principle is not modified by the island theory. The island theory (or net investment concept) treats certain risks which might otherwise appear as short-term risks as parts of a wider and longer-term risk, but this conceptual change affects both true and

140

accounting concepts. It will only make a difference if it causes companies to treat subsidiaries as islands which on a true view of the risk they would decide to regard as more fragmented separate risks with different maturities. But this again is not likely to be a common occurrence.

Our startling conclusion, therefore, is that if we assume current value accounting, and a defensive approach to risk management, and a realization that currency exposures managed as transaction risks will effectively also be neutralized as accounting risks, there will in practice be very few cases of conflict between managing true risk and managing accounting risk. Moreover, this surprising conclusion holds for the temporal method and ED 21 as well as for the two exposure drafts of 1980.

Assuming historic cost accounting

When we drop the assumption that the basic accounting has been done at current values, then we get a very different picture. We can shorten this discussion by restricting it to either fixed assets or islands which include fixed assets. A more detailed discussion in Chapter 18 showed that these are the main problems.

To put it in a nutshell, a true view of our risk requires us to match the true value of fixed assets with borrowings of *equal magnitude* in the same currency (assuming for this purpose that all other net assets in the currency balance out to zero). To compute the amount of debt we need to bring our true exposure to zero, we use the true value of the fixed assets, not their historic balance sheet values. We reached this conclusion in Chapter 18 after considering and for practical purposes rejecting the view that fixed assets, due to the operation of the purchasing power parity relationship, do not constitute an exposure at all and therefore should not be financed by matching currency debt. And we also reached the view that for practical purposes true value can be equated with current value.

The accounting conflicts can be illustrated by the following example:

Example 25

An American company has a British subsidiary with the following (historic cost) balance sheet

	£000		£000
Share capital	10	Fixed assets (current	
Reserves	50	value 2800)	1200
Payables	450	Inventories	1000
£ overdraft	50	Receivables	900
$ loan	2600	Cash	60
	£3160		£3160

Note: there is no significant difference between the historic and current values of the inventories.

Using these data, we get the following different views of the sterling exposure of the US parent:

True risk: £4 260 000 (equity 10 + 50 = 60 + $ debt 2600 + undervaluation of fixed assets 1600)

FAS 8 risk: £1 460 000 (current assets 1960 less £ liabilities 500). If we had not assumed that the inventories are at current values, the risk would be £460 000.

ED 21 risk: £2 660 000 (true risk 4260 less overvaluation 1600). The parent under ED 21 could neutralize the risk by borrowing £2 660 000 sterling.

ED 27 risk: £2 660 000 again (unless temporal method applies), but the parent can only use the cover method to the extent of the net investment of £60 000 by borrowing sterling. If the parent borrowed the whole £2 660 000, the excess amount of £2 600 000 would constitute a short position in its own accounts. This could cause a loss before tax to the US parent. The corresponding gain on the UK company's long position would go to reserve!

US draft August 1980: as for ED 27.

Accounting definition of balance sheet risk

We defined true balance sheet risk in Chapter 20. Accounting risk is harder to define in general terms because its precise character must depend on the particular accounting convention which happens to apply. It also needs to distinguish between the effect of gains or losses on the profit and loss account, or even various lines in that account under some conventions.

The definition is the following:

Balance sheet risk in accounting terms is the risk to a company or a group of companies which has an imbalance between exposed assets and liabilities in any currency other than its reporting currency, of a loss in its income before tax, on other lines of its income statement, or in other parts of its net worth as displayed in its individual or consolidated financial statements, from any adverse movement between that currency and the reporting currency from the exchange rate at the previous balance sheet date or from the rate at which the item concerned was first recorded in the books during the current period. The risk is separate for each accounting period, and the gains and losses from it are measured in accordance with the accounting conventions used for the company or group. In this definition 'exposed' assets or liabilities include those bought or sold forward for the currency concerned, but not those originally denominated in it and sold or bought forward for another currency; they have become part of the exposure in that latter currency. 'Exposed' assets and liabilities also include postnatal trading or similar commitments which are not yet visible on a balance sheet. They exclude, however, any assets or liabilities which the accounting convention in force requires to be translated at an unvarying exchange rate over the years.

How different is accounting risk?

Our review therefore suggests that an accounting view of balance sheet risk makes a major difference to its management, but mainly where fixed assets are shown at historic values in the basic accounts. There is also the problem of whether we manage with an eye on the next balance sheet date or on the ultimate life-span of the risk, but that can be overcome because the latter view, which treats it as a transaction risk, automatically also deals with the risk at intervening accounting dates. And there is the problem under the 1980 exposure drafts that all translation differences in a single company become part of the ordinary profit or loss before tax, but the difference which this will make to actual management action may be fairly limited.

No, the worst failure of the accounting conventions in harmonizing the accounting view of risk with the true nature of risk is in not merging the topics of translation and inflation accounting. This omission seems to be deliberate, for we read in paragraph 84 of the FASB exposure draft: 'The Board believes resolution of inflation-related issues should not be considered as part of the Board's deliberations on foreign currency translation'.

ED 27, it is true, says that in countries with very high rates of inflation ('hyperinflation'), it may be necessary to revalue fixed assets in the local currency financial statements before the translation process is undertaken. But the principle applies equally in countries with less high inflation rates. In any case the American draft of August 1980 was published after deleting even this limited concession to the cause of harmonization.

But perhaps this is a temporary problem. If in due course we can look to the universal adoption of some form of current value accounting, then the major source of possible conflict between true and accounting risk management will have faded away.

The final choice

But in the meantime we have a dilemma between the two approaches to the management of balance sheet risk wherever we have fixed assets standing in the accounts at historic values and wherever a group is either reluctant or unable to balance its currency positions in each group company. The choice is one of objectives, and it is not an easy one. No responsible board of directors can lightly ignore the way in which the company reports its results and net worth, let alone adopt a policy which risks the appearance of losses in the financial statements, even if that policy protects the true net worth and equity stake of the shareholders. At the same time the opposite policy of taking a risk with the true value of the net worth can hardly be defended either. One example of this, as we saw in an earlier chapter, is the sudden liquidity crisis in which we have to realize our investment in a subsidiary at short notice. If the board have managed the accounting exposure rather than the true risk, this could lock the company into a permanent loss.

To illustrate, we look again at Example 25. If we assume a 10% fall in sterling before the US parent has to sell the subsidiary soon after its balance sheet date, there will be no realized loss if the parent borrowed £4.26 million, a loss of £160 000 (10% of £1.6 million) if it borrowed £2.66 million despite the different way in which the 1980 exposure drafts treat gains and losses on the parent's borrowing and the subsidiary's net sterling assets in excess of net worth; and finally a loss of £420 000 (10% of £4.2 million) if the parent company borrowed only £60 000 because that was the size of the net investment available for the cover method.

So the choice between managing the accounting risk or the true risk is not a matter of taking the long or the short view. Even on the short view it is not safe to ignore the true risk. Not without misgivings therefore, we must ultimately come down on the side of managing the true risk if we cannot harmonize the two concepts. When the chips are down, we may have to give it preference over the accounting view of risk. It may be, however, that the accounting world will soon give us translation conventions which, together with current value accounting, will deliver companies from the dilemma.

PART 6

The Remaining Problems of Managing
Balance Sheet Risks

CHAPTER 22

Currency Risk and Interest Rates

The relationship between inflation, currency movements and interest rates

Several times in this book we have come across the fact that the forward premium or discount approximates to the difference between the Euro-currency interest rates for funds in the same two currencies for the same period, both expressed as a percentage per annum. In Chapter 18 we mentioned the Fisher Open theorem which suggests that market arbitrage will operate to bring the per annum difference between the two Eurocurrency interest rates to the *expected* per annum movement in the spot rate over the same period. For if the market failed to do that, there would be an opportunity to make a profit by switching funds to the currency which gives the higher return after covering forward the amount of the principal. In practice the forward rate and the interest differential are poor forecasts of future spot rates. No doubt this indicates that market expectations of those movements tend to be inaccurate when measured against the out-turn.

This is not to dispute the fact that currency movements and interest rates have a correlation; the doubt concerns which is cause and which the effect. Governments sometimes try to manipulate exchange rates by means of pushing interest rates up or down. At other times interest rates adjust to the market's view of the relative strength of different currencies, as the Fisher Open theorem suggests.

It is useful to think of interest rates as consisting of two elements: the expected real rate of interest and the expected inflation rate. This relationship is known as the Fisher Closed theorem (Aliber, op.cit. p.31). If real interest rates are relatively stable, this implies a close correlation between the rate of interest and the expected rate of inflation. We have already in chapters 6 and 18 observed the relationship between currency movements and relative rates of inflation. We can therefore now note that inflation, interest rates and exchange rates are interlinked by a trio of instructive interrelationships.

Example 26   Brazil

The Brazilian inflation rate declined from 85% in 1964 to about 15% in 1973, and then by 1980 rose back to above 100%. The cruzeiro has typically fallen against the US dollar by the difference between the US and Brazilian inflation rates, but in 1976–79 the cruzeiro was devalued less fast until in December 1979 it had to catch up with a maxidevaluation of 30%.

The only free market for cruzeiro funds is the 'investment' market, mainly for 90-day and 180-day notes. Rates in this market have fluctuated up and down with the rate of inflation, leaving sometimes a negative, sometimes a positive real interest rate. In Brazil it is often hard to know whether inflation is going up or down, because the indices are published several months in arrears. Consequently there may be a wide margin between expected rates of inflation and actual rates. Typically if the inflation rate is 100%, investment market funds cost a little more than 100%, and if the rate of inflation in the United States is (say) 12%, devaluation against the dollar would normally be about 88% per annum. The only alternative source of free market funds are United States dollars. If Eurodollars cost 12%, various taxes and other costs raise this to an effective rate between 15% and 20%, and the remaining difference between the cruzeiro cost of dollars and the cost of cruzeiro investment market funds is the expected rate of devaluation against the dollar. The market evidently through arbitrage equates the effective cost of the two sources of funds in cruzeiros, and that effective cost fluctuates quite sharply up and down with the inflation rate.

In this example we assume that we are a US parent company whose Brazilian subsidiary last year bought a property for Cr3 000 000, which was then the equivalent of $100 000. This year the book value is still Cr3 000 000, but after 100% inflation its current value is now Cr6.0 million = $100 000 (ignoring US inflation). But the subsidiary financed the purchase by borrowing Cr3.0 million in the investment market. Now a year later this debt is worth only $50 000. So have we somehow gained $50 000? The point is not about accounting methods. Both the rent-earning capacity and the replacement cost of the asset are likely to have doubled in cruzeiros but remained still in dollars, but the debt has halved in purchasing power and dollar terms. No, we have not gained any significant amount, for we are likely to have paid interest on the debt at about 100%, nearly all of it as the price of inflation. In the accounts, however, the whole of that cost will show up as interest expense. Now suppose the Brazilian company had borrowed $100 000 instead of Cr3 million to buy the land, then the annual combined cost of the dollar interest, withholding taxes, etc., and the unrealized loss on the principal amount of the borrowing due to the fall of the cruzeiro against the dollar, would probably also have amounted to about Cr3 000 000. But in this total the unrealized currency loss is likely to be much the largest item. The accounts will treat this as an exchange loss. It is clearly uninformative in these circumstances that the accounts will treat the effects of alternative financing methods so differently. In essence the phenomena of inflation, devaluation and interest are so closely intertwined that any arbitrary distinction between their effects is unrealistic. Even Brazilian tax law allows this type of unrealized exchange loss as a deductible expense for arriving at taxable profit, just as if it had been an interest expense.

Interest and forward cover

We have already noted the causal relation between forward rates and the difference between interest rates in the currencies concerned, and that only minor gains can usually be made by switching from (say) sterling to French franc debt in the Eurocurrency markets and covering them forward. The jargon calls this 'covered arbitrage'. We have also noted in Chapter 9 that forward cover can have a negative cost—indeed the cost must be negative for one or the other party to a forward contract. These features have led quite a few people to think of forward cover less as a form of insurance than as an interest-related transaction. They regard the process of selling D-marks forward for US dollars as a decision to finance in D-marks rather than in US dollars. The perception is useful and illuminating, but it is no more than part of the truth. The forward contract can also be used, and is perhaps normally used, so as to convert an uncertainty into a certainty (as regards the currency outcome of a transaction), and to that extent is quite properly viewed as an insurance against loss.

We have seen that in many circumstances a currency borrowing does exactly the same job at exactly the same positive or negative cost. But before we decide that we are indifferent between the two hedging devices, we must of course check the tax effect of each of them. This could be different. It could for example turn on whether the item covered forward is itself regarded as capital or revenue for tax purposes.

Forward cover as a fixed interest transaction

A forward contract is of course an implied fixed interest deal. If a bank buys dollars forward from us for a date 3 years from now, the bank will hedge the deal by borrowing dollars for 3 years and depositing sterling for 3 years, both at fixed rates of interest, and it will pay to us as our premium the difference between its dollar interest cost and the (assumed higher) interest earnings on the sterling deposit, less its margin. The bank can do all this because there is an interbank market in dollars and sterling at fixed rates of interest, which stretches as far as 3 years.

But the fixed interest interbank market may not stretch beyond 3 years; and in some other currencies the longest maturities might be 12 or 6 months. And these limits are also the limits of the reach of the forward markets. The limits vary of course from time to time, and the only point which we are concerned to make here is that the stretch of the forward markets is governed by the stretch of the fixed rate interbank markets for funds in the currencies concerned.

We have found that forward cover and currency borrowings are the two most useful hedging devices. Borrowings are perhaps the most useful of the two devices against balance sheet risks. But we have now found that in the bank markets both of them are available for only restricted periods. Fixed rate money from banks and forward contracts are practically never available for more than 5 years. In the non-bank markets, especially in the bond markets we can, of course, raise fixed interest money for longer periods; indeed in those markets we might have difficulty in getting maturities of less than 10 years. But a bond issue takes time to mount, and may not be a convenient means of hedging a currency risk; for that often needs to be done in a matter of hours.

But the interesting and important qualification in all this is that it is only *fixed interest* debt for which the bank market is so restricted in the various currencies. If we cared to borrow at variable rates, perhaps with a 6-monthly rollover covenant, a bank is usually willing to accept a commitment for much longer periods, often up to 10 or more years. The major constraint has been removed.

If we have an excess of assets over liabilities in a currency with a known or assessed life of between (say) 5 and 10 years, and if we can only borrow that currency for 1 or 3 years, then we have to take a chance on being able to refinance at maturity in the same currency, or accept debt at variable rates of interest.

Variable interest borrowings are likely to give the debtor a good bargain. Since the 1950s interest rates have become so volatile that lenders are less and less willing to lend funds which are both unindexed and priced at relatively low fixed rates of interest. A borrower who gets just one of those two features is still doing well. What the borrower must assess is whether the risk of paying that much more interest over the years is better or worse than the risk of losing on the principal if he leaves the currency exposure unhedged. This choice obviously brings in the tax and accounting dimensions. It is quite possible that in most cases the variable interest risk is less painful. If it is, then the variable interest covenant is the better choice.

The detailed terms are obviously important here. With floating rate debt the borrower should normally be able to obtain the right to prepay without penalty or to have a one-sided multicurrency option in case he should wish to sell the asset or avoid excessive interest costs.

But the main lesson here is that in many cases a longer term is preferable to a fixed interest covenant.

The interest rate trap

We first came upon this phenomenon in Example 21 in Chapter 17. It is now a commonplace that well-known companies and UK nationalized industries badly burnt their fingers in the early 1970s by borrowing Swiss francs and other strong currencies at temptingly low rates of interest. Some well-known companies went under as a result. The decisions which turned out to be so disastrous were in some cases encouraged by financial advisers and bankers. It is fair to remember that most of these decisions were taken before the Bretton Woods system had finally broken down and therefore before a really steep rise in (say) the Swiss franc was generally recognized as a possibility.

There is of course a great deal wrong with a policy of saving interest by accepting a currency exposure:

1. It must be wrong to focus excessive attention on interest rates and to neglect the burden of the repayment obligation.
2. Under most systems of taxation, the interest burden is fully tax-deductable whereas under many of them a loss on the repayment liability is not allowable for tax. Even if we believe that the difference between their interest rates expresses the market's expectation of the future movement in the exchange rate between two currencies (that is, the Fisher Open), that theorem does not purport to describe the effect after tax.
3. In any case, the Fisher Open theorem does not purport to predict exchange rate movements. It merely asserts that the difference between interest rate levels will adjust to expected changes in the exchange rate. In real life currencies move with greater volatility than interest rates.
4. Whether we are in sympathy with the accounting conventions or not, we cannot disregard them. For they have powerful consequences. For example, the interest saving boosts the earnings which cover the dividend. The shareholders may therefore press for the distribution of those extra earnings, even if they are balanced or exceeded by a capital loss which under some accounting conventions (like ED 21, but not under FAS 8 or the 1980 US and UK exposure drafts) does not reduce earnings. This could help to erode a company's ability to meet the repayment obligation. The directors in a case like that would of course watch the overall effect on net worth.

So we cannot support the interest rate trap. It cannot be correct to borrow the currency with the cheapest interest cost, simply because of the low rate of interest. But there seem to be two rival schools of thought about what we should do instead. One view is that we should simply match assets and liabilities in each non-reporting currency, that is, borrow whatever currency our assets are in. The other view (see J. A. Donaldson, 1980, p. 96 with special reference to non-monetary assets) believes that we must not do this if it means borrowing a hard currency.

It would of course be a caricature of both schools if we described them as regarding interest rates as wholly immaterial. If our corporate objective were to maximize net worth by any means, whether through the income statement or through reserves, and if we *knew* that the lower cost after tax of borrowing a certain hard currency would outweigh the currency loss on the principal, then we should of course borrow the currency with the lower interest cost.

What is in doubt is whether we could ever know that. Experience tends to show that the loss on the principal normally exceeds the interest saving before, let alone after, tax. So how can we ever be sure that a particular decision will succeed against all normal experience?

The school which is merely against borrowing hard currencies is on firmer ground, but here we come back to the difficulty we found in Chapter 18 of identifying hard currencies. The D-mark and Swiss franc have a long-standing track record of hardness, most third-world currencies (other than the OPEC ones) and the Italian lira and the peseta seem to be endemically soft, but it would not be easy to call the dollar, the French franc, sterling or yen, for example, reliably hard or soft. Moreover, the lesson of the 1970s seems to be that changes in status do occur and that all currencies are getting less predictable.

In these circumstances it seems sensible to conclude that non-financial companies at any rate should aim to have a capability to control their affairs at a zero level of risk, and to take deliberate and calculated departures from this risk-neutral norm to the extent that their corporate attitudes, philosophies and objectives prompt them to do this.

If that is the correct principle, then the answer to the interest trap problem must be that all companies should have a normal rule to match assets and liabilities in the same currency, irrespective of whether other currencies would be cheaper to borrow. Moreover, they should prefer a risk on variable interest rates to a risk or loss on the principal. That is the norm. However, provided that a company clearly has the appropriate corporate objectives and the professional capability to control deliberate exposures, it may well decide to depart from this norm if it sees a chance to take a professionally assessed and managed risk by borrowing what it believes to be a weaker currency than the currency which would match the excess net assets. This formulation seems to accommodate both schools of thought, the 'matching' school and the 'never borrow strong currencies' school. It means of course in most cases that any departures from a policy of matching everything are likely to be towards borrowing a currency with a higher, rather than a lower, cost of money.

Reference

Donaldson, J. A. (1980). *Corporate Currency Risk*, The Financial Times Business Information Ltd., London.

CHAPTER 23

When to Hedge and for What Maturities

In this chapter we look at the maturity problems of hedging balance sheet risks, and at the timing problems. These two sets of problems are among the greatest headaches in currency risk management. We assume throughout, as always, that our company has a normal rule to avoid or hedge all risks (from which it may decide to take controlled departures).

Three types of situation

In Chapter 20 we examined when balance sheet risk begins. In that process we distinguished three different types of beginnings, or at any rate perceived beginnings:

* First, there is the case of a clear-cut significant fresh acquisition or other investment, like the purchase of a new Belgian subsidiary.
* Second, there is the major review of our currency equilibrium, often after a period of neglect.
* Third, there is the periodic updating of this review so as to catch up with the inevitable organic change in the picture which goes on all the time in a dynamic business.

For what maturities do we aim to hedge?

In the case of the new Belgian subsidiary we have the advantage that we can usually make our financing decision for the purchase with an eye on what liability will best hedge the risk. So if the purchase results in a simple addition of net Belgian franc assets, and our previous group balance in Belgian francs was a net zero position, then we can simply borrow Belgian francs to finance the purchase. We can do this even if the purchaser wants to be paid in US dollars; we borrow Belgian francs and sell them spot for US dollars. Then if we regard the new subsidiary as an 'island', and a permanent part of the group, we put a life of (say) 25 or 30 years on the asset and look for Belgian franc funds with that maturity. We may not find funds for that long a period; this is a point to which we return later in this chapter. But in principle we want to borrow Belgian francs for 25 or 30 years.

The case of the major review is much more difficult. Many such reviews occurred particularly in the 1970s when companies gradually came to realize that floating currencies had come to stay, and that the stability of the Bretton Woods era will not return in the foreseeable future. A major review of this kind often discloses a chaotic picture, with many imbalances. Some of these will be in individual companies of the group, some in the group as a whole. They will have all kinds of different maturities. Some will be positive (more assets than liabilities in a currency), some negative. What we have to do is to sort the imbalances out in each currency and to subdivide them by maturities. We must identify the islands and allocate maturities to the non-monetary assets and liabilities outside those islands, adjusting for items covered forward and including postnatal commitments not yet on the balance sheet. The resulting matrix shows what hedging action needs to be taken: it does not tell us when it should be taken: that is the timing problem to which we come at the end of this chapter.

Supposing for the moment that we have got our position balanced, we then come to the third situation in which we find at regular reviews that imbalances have reappeared in the ordinary course of business and perhaps even through the evolution of the external environment. Fortunately these organic deviations from a position which was balanced not so long ago are not often very large, and can usually be corrected by fairly minor hedging action. It is seldom necessary to undertake these updating reviews very frequently, say more than once a year, when we look at internal dividend policy. But the interval will vary from company to company. Nor is it possible to generalize about the maturities for which we should hedge the imbalances that come to light in such a review. We have to consider the size and maturity structure of the imbalance, the forward and money markets in the currency, and the trend of that currency in the market. If it has a clear tendency to rise or fall, rather than fluctuate, or if it has a thin market like the Malaysian ringgit, it may be best to match out even small maturities when the opportunity arises. But in many cases it may pay us to treat minor imbalances from such fluctuations as temporary, and to keep our positions flexible, which means reversible. Any major long-term restructuring is best done when we can see a clear, substantial and persistent imbalance, probably after more than one regular review period.

The case where we cannot get long enough maturities

At the beginning of this chapter we said that if we see the new Belgian subsidiary as an island to which we attribute a long life of (say) 25 or 30 years, then we should be looking for Belgian francs to borrow for 25 or 30 years. Obviously, if our corporate objectives were preoccupied with the accounting rather than the true risk, our policy would be modified along the lines discussed in Chapter 21.

But what if we can only hedge for 12 years because funds are not available to us in Belgian francs for any longer—not even at variable rates of interest (a point we looked at in Chapter 22)? This is a very real problem. If our estimated asset life of 25 or 30 years is only an arbitrary assessment, so that a much shorter commercial life of 12 years is also possible, then it will not worry us much. But the more certain we are that the asset life is longer, the less sure we are that Belgian francs can be borrowed in 12 years' time, the greater must be our reluctance to accept that limit of 12 years. We shall obviously do our best to look for back-to-back or parallel loans or bilateral swaps of longer maturities than 12 years. But at the end of the day if 12 years is the longest protection we can get, we must take it rather than take anything still shorter.

But a dilemma between 12-year and 25 or 30-year Belgian francs is not the worst that can occur!

Example 27   Investing in Spain

We have invested in a manufacturing company in Spain at a cost of Pts72 million. We are an American company, and the investment cost us $1 million. The investment should have a market life of at least 15 years, but we can only borrow pesetas for 3 years. In order to use the pesetas as a hedge, we have to sell them for dollars, which we do at the acquisition spot rate of Pts72 = $1. On maturity we find we cannot roll over, because the market for pesetas has dried up, and we have to pay $1 200 000 at Pts60 = $1 to meet our repayment obligation. We have made a *cash* loss of $200 000, and are now fully exposed with no hedge.

This of course is again an extreme example to illustrate the problems of inadequately hedged maturities. A short while ago we did not find it necessarily disastrous to take a chance and cover part of our Belgian franc risk with an assumed life of 30 years for only 12 years. Why do we think differently about the gap between 3 years and 15 years in the case of the Spanish peseta? The differences are:

1. The Belgian franc has a better track record of marketability than the peseta. The chance of finding no offshore funds at some future date is greater in the case of the peseta.
2. 12 years and 30 years are both long maturities from where we are now in year 1, whereas 3 and 15 years are different *orders* of maturities. One is at the short end of the medium term, the other is firmly in the long term. 3 years is within current planning spans, 15 years

is not. We do not really know whether the product or activity will be obsolete in 12, 15 or 30 years, but we ought to have a very sharp idea about 3 years from now.

There are some very highly respected currencies which can cause more severe problems of this kind than the peseta. The Australian dollar is among them. This is not a problem to which there are easy answers. Currency problems are only one part of the economic environment in which we have to make our decisions. But before we invest in the country of a not very marketable currency, we must pause and consider whether the currency and political risks are worth the attractions of the project. We deal with this general topic of currencies with poor marketability in the next chapter.

When to hedge

The maturity problem can be difficult, but the timing problem can be downright impossible.

The nature of this problem must not be misunderstood. If our company adopts the attitude advocated in this book, and normally refuses to accept currency risks, then the normal policy will of course be to hedge all risks at birth. If we are acquiring a new Belgian subsidiary, then we should aim to pay for the acquisition by borrowing Belgian francs. In that case there is no timing problem.

But as we saw, some risks appear when we review our currency positions, possibly after a long period of neglect. In that case we must expect to find very large risks, that is, very large imbalances between assets and liabilities in various currencies. Now did we by any chance come to conduct this major review because our accounts for the last year or two had shown translation losses big enough to cause us some concern? And in that case were the losses perhaps due to an unusually long and steep rise in the value of our parent reporting currency against the other currencies in which we have group assets? Even if that is what has happened, we should see no timing problem if our parent currency is the D-mark or the Swiss franc whose strength we may have good reason to see as long-term. If we report in such a strong currency, then we should without further delay borrow the currencies against which our currency is so persistently rising to the detriment of our consolidated equity. But if our parent currency is the yen, the US dollar, sterling, or the French franc, none of which have been free from ups and downs, then we should pause before we jump in and borrow the other currencies which have recently been falling against our parent currency. We should pause to ask whether the present moment is felicitous for borrowing so as to neutralize the imbalances. For with hindsight we could be seen to have stabilized the position near the very top of the upswing in our currency, and just before the heavy accounting losses of the past few years were about to reverse themselves. And if our stockholders saw that we locked ourselves into those losses near their peak, they may think our timing less than adroit, however much they may welcome our determination to prevent further risks to their investment.

The problem is, of course, that we cannot possibly be certain whether our parent currency is near the peak of its rise. On the other hand our neglect of the exposure up to now may well have rested on some explicit or implicit belief that the recent trend would not be permanent. In that belief we might well have been correct, even if we failed to realize the depth of the possible swings in the currency and the magnitude of the effects on our net worth. We may, therefore, not unfairly, be expected to time our transition from a policy of unmanaged risk to one of total risk neutrality (if that is what we have now decided we need) in a reasonable manner, and not to do it at the worst possible phase in the cyclical pattern of our currency. The fact that we cannot predict the turning point in the market does not excuse us from using all the professional expertise that we can command in making our judgement about that timing. The idea of changing from a risky to a riskless policy is good, but it does not excuse us from exercising great care and skill in making the change.

The dilemma which we have just discussed is of course closely related to the dilemma to which we have already referred in Chapter 16, where we quoted J A Donaldson's point that in the life of every exposure there must be 'an optimum moment at which to make the deal'. If we want to clean up a balance sheet riddled with risks hitherto unmanaged, we can get by with doing the deal at almost anything better than the *worst* moment. But the trouble with all risks which we fail to hedge at birth is that we are in the unenviable position that whatever we do thereafter, it is a 99% safe bet that it will turn out with hindsight that we could have done better. We saw this in Chapter 13 when we discussed the netting matrix method. There is really no such thing as a single choice whether to hedge or not. We can arbitrarily create such a choice by institutionalizing a formal monthly or weekly review of every short and long position. We then have a 'yes or no' choice, and on maturity of each risk we can monitor with hindsight whether we picked the right horse in a two-horse race between the forward and the spot rate, and compute the percentage success of our decisions. Indeed, it is hard to see how else we can make our task manageable. But the fact is that it is not a two-horse race. It is a race with as many horses as there are forward rates at which we could do the deal between now and maturity, and our two-horse monitoring system does not even ascertain whether our horse was in the top half of the field.

In practice we can slightly improve upon the monthly 'yes/no' decision by setting ourselves at each such meeting a hurdle forward rate. This is a definite instruction to our dealers to do the currency deal whenever a forward rate becomes available in the market which is as favourable to us or better than the hurdle rate. This will not ensure that we pick the winning horse, or even a horse in the top half of the field. On the contrary, it could lock us into a deal which with *hindsight* will look far from optimal. We might, for example, turn out to have backed the slowest horse in an exceptionally fast race. But at least it forces us into the discipline of making a professional judgement of what is an acceptable time for the course. We shall between monthly reviews do the deal if we can get it at a rate which in our best judgement we should be able to attain if we are neither greedy nor too unambitious. The effort and the judgement which we have to put into that assessment is more appropriate to the seriousness of the issue.

In Chapters 14 and 19 we concluded that trading risks not hedged or managed by the time of birth, had to be managed as balance sheet risks. We now find that balance sheet risks involve these difficult timing puzzles which are responsible for so many stomach ulcers in the world of treasurers. All balance sheet risk management involves this nerve-fraying trauma, and ex-trading risks merely add to the size and to the number of maturities of this problem; they do not cause it. Currency risk tends to be steep in a regime of floating currencies, and any decision or non-decision which results in acceptance of a postnatal unhedged exposure can only be justified if we are willing and able to deploy the considerable skill needed to do better than hedging at birth. The only possible vindication is success. Needless to add, all this amounts to a formidable case against taking on the risks, and leaving them unhedged, in the first place.

So our conclusions on this difficult topic are: The right time to hedge significant new exposures is at birth. Where significant risks are not discovered until later, that is, in the postnatal stage, we should pause before we take hedging action, and consider whether there is good reason to postpone action. If immediate action looks as if it might be very poor timing, we should not only arrange frequent and regular reviews, but also give the dealer a hurdle exchange rate (for the maturity or for each maturity) at which he should deal and take hedging action if the opportunity arises. If in doubt we should hedge sooner rather than later.

CHAPTER 24

Political Risk and Tax Problems

Restrictions on companies

The management of balance sheet risk is often impeded or constrained by exchange controls and other restrictions. Some of these can apply in the country of the parent company. A company seeking to balance its currency position by borrowings, by the use of forward cover, operating currency bank accounts, investing outside the country or lending to non-residents, leading and lagging trade credit, or adjusting intercompany prices so as to shift margins and cash between currency areas, may find itself severely constrained in respect of some or all of these devices by exchange controls operated by its own government. This would certainly be true of a parent company in Italy or South Africa, and these are relatively liberal countries in economic matters.

In the above list we refer to adjusting intercompany prices. There used to be quite a vogue for advising companies to use this technique, as well as charging internal management fees, adjusting internal cross-frontier interest rates at almost any level from nil to twice the commercial rate, and charging royalties and other service charges for services rendered, with the aim of influencing internal profits and cash flow between countries. These topics have become much less fashionable mainly because the governments whose regulations these devices were designed to circumvent, have become more and more sophisticated at frustrating them, and partly no doubt because groups of companies found that the internal management, administration and motivation consequences of these efforts were not worth the benefits. But more important from our point of view in this book, these particular devices must be looked upon as affecting the international distribution of profits and tax liabilities much more than the cash and currency positions. In practice it is very rare to find an opportunity to use one of them as a currency management weapon as such.

So far we have looked at possible restrictions in our parent company's home base. An even greater problem are restrictions imposed in the countries where the subsidiaries operate. In addition to the restrictions which we can find in our home base, we can here be restricted or penally taxed in paying dividends (as well as royalties, management fees and interest), repatriating capital, repaying intercompany loans, shortening or even excessively lengthening intercompany credit, access to local funds, forward markets, and just about everything we might wish to do to protect our currency position. Governments can make the local currency less than fully convertible, prevent the development of an efficient offshore market for the currency, make non-local currency borrowings subject to penal interest-free deposits with the central bank, and create bureaucratic delays for all remittances of foreign currency. These are just a few of the possible restrictions and impediments. There is really no end to the ingenuity of those who wish to interfere with free currency markets.

The sad fact is that there are only a handful of currencies with completely free and efficient markets, so that investment in the majority of countries is to varying degrees exposed to these hazards.

Most of the problems created by these restrictions are outside the scope of this book, like the problem of justifying the investment of group shareholders' funds in a country from which not even profits, let alone capital can be freely repatriated.

What does concern us are the constraints on our efforts to avoid or hedge balance sheet currency exposures. For example, the limited benefit of leading and lagging is reduced to vanishing point if the subsidiary cannot finance any reduction of the internal credit from local borrowings, or if the local regulations forbid faster payment. Even our primary weapon for managing the balance sheet, borrowing local currencies, is frustrated if the currency cannot be borrowed either locally or offshore.

Pure political risk

So far we have only spoken of financial or economic risks. Now suppose we also have grounds for worrying about purely political measures. For example, whether our local operation might be confiscated, occupied by irregular authorities, or nationalized, or denied access to vital local resources or markets. In such cases, if we invest at all, we should of course aim to finance the local activity as far as possible from local debt and without guarantees from elsewhere in the group. This does not directly affect currency risk management, but it affects it indirectly because in this type of case the group cannot be indifferent whether it borrows the local currency in the local subsidiary, or offshore in another country. The local subsidiary must be the borrower.

The parallel hedge

Some authorities advocate the use of the parallel hedge to overcome the problem where a currency is not available to be borrowed offshore. For example, borrowing D-marks instead of Austrian schillings, or perhaps Singapore dollars instead of Malaysian ringgits. The markets for both schillings and ringgits have at times been thin and difficult to tap. It is not nearly as safe to borrow the 'parallel' currency as the actual currency in which we have excess assets. The assumption that the schilling cannot get badly out of line with the D-mark or that the ringgit cannot move far from parity with the Singapore dollar is by no means safe. The mere fact that one central bank is determined to manage its currency close to parity with another, can imply a willingness to operate *against* market forces, which can in the long run build up so large a disequilibrium that the dam must burst and a major adjustment replace the smooth functioning of the normal market ups and downs. Nevertheless, a parallel hedge in a case like this may well be better than nothing. But much less defensible is the time-honoured practice of ignoring the fact that a Canadian dollar is not a US dollar, or an Irish punt not a pound sterling. Not only has experience taught us that major fluctuations are common between these pairs of currencies, but there is no excuse for treating them as parallel hedges as there are perfectly free markets in the Canadian and Irish currencies.

The effect of taxation

This book is not about taxation, but we have had to make repeated references to the tax effect of various hedging actions. Taxation is a specialized subject with its own specialist literature, and it is clear that in particular the subject of whether currency gains or losses on borrowings are taxable or tax-deductible (as the case may be) is difficult, is likely to vary from country to country and often between different types of gains or losses in the tax law of a single given country. For example in the United Kingdom a gain or loss on repayment of a currency debt incurred in the normal course of trade, would be treated as part of the taxable profit of the company. On the other hand, if the debt had been incurred for a purely capital purpose or transaction, the gain or loss would probably be ignored for the purpose of computing taxable profits.

But that leaves other possibilities, such as whether such a gain or loss would affect the taxation of capital gains rather than trading income. In the United Kingdom, for example, foreign currency as such is a chargeable asset subject to tax on capital gains, but UK tax law does not contemplate any tax effect in this context from gains or losses on a liability.

Brazil is an example of a country where losses on foreign currency liabilities reduce taxable profits. Interest is in most cases taxable in the hands of the recipient and allowable in the case of the payer as a reduction of taxable income. This obviously depends on the tax position of the company, and there are many exceptions like withholding taxes to these general rules. Wherever the effect of interest is reduced by tax at the corporation tax rate, this is a reinforcement of the tendency for the effect of interest and interest rates to be less critical than the effect of hedging on the principal amount at risk. But all generalizations here are dangerous. There are no prizes for the treasurer who does not do his detailed homework case by case on his various options.

These are just a few examples of the variety of rules which can be encountered in the field of taxation. We must, however, end with a further reminder that governments can use tax as a powerful weapon against unwelcome currency operations. The swingeing Brazilian tax on dividends is an example. It virtually prevents repatriation of profits from Brazil, and is the most powerful legal disincentive to investment in that country.

Tax effect on amount of hedge needed

If we use forward cover (not always the best device for balance sheet hedging anyway) against a balance sheet exposure in conditions where the outcome of the forward contract will affect taxable profit but the risk hedged will not (for example, because the imbalance of net assets in the currency is located in a foreign subsidiary), the amount required to cover the risk *after tax* is not the amount of the imbalance, but $100/(100 - t)$ of it, where t is the marginal rate of tax on the gain or loss on the forward contract. Where we use forward cover in this way, this point needs to be watched.

CHAPTER 25

The Issues of Balance Sheet Risk Management Reviewed

The time has come to pull together the various threads which we have followed ever since Chapter 18. We assume in general that we are describing a group of companies which wants to know how to attain something close to zero exposure, irrespective of how far (if at all) it may then decide to make some aggressive departures from it. We also assume all the definitions that we have adopted in this book, and in particular that all risks, even those which began as trading risks, should be managed as part of the balance sheet problem once they remain unhedged after birth.

Currency risk management in perspective

First of all, currency risk management cannot become the tail that wags the dog. Currency risk is part of the business environment, but seldom the most important part of it. Currency considerations cannot take precedence over the need to sell products at a profit, the need to attack certain markets, or the legal and tax legislation with which we have to live, the requirements of the stock market in which we raise our capital and so on. Currency considerations will contribute to the view we take of all these, but so must other considerations.

For example, to correct an excess of Swiss franc liabilities over assets, we are not likely to start a 'green field' manufacturing project in Switzerland so as to balance our currency position, if Swiss manufacturing costs are unlikely to be competitive in the world market. Again, if we wish to reduce our net position in French francs, we should be ill-advised to adjust transfer prices between our French company and the rest of the group if this will entail unrelieved tax losses in France (and create taxable profits elsewhere), or jeopardize the solvency of the French subsidiary, or even demotivate the local management in France. It can very seldom be right to use pricing as a currency management tool; prices have too many other, usually more critical, implications.

Currency implications are likely to have a much greater influence on financing decisions. After all, the whole topic of balance sheet currency risk management is part of the wider topic of financing. But even here we have to be careful. If we need to add to our liabilities in (say) guilders, we must ponder whether the extra debt will cause a breach of a restriction in a debenture trust deed or in the company's articles of association or constitution. We should also be aware that if we borrow a currency other than the one in which the restrictions are defined, that currency can float up so as to break the restriction at a later date. The act of borrowing is primarily a financing activity, and its use for currency risk management must not cause conflict with general financing policy.

There is, of course, often a technical way round this last problem. If we want to borrow guilders and have cash deposits in another currency, perhaps we could so arrange things that both are with the same bank and covered by an agreement conferring upon both parties the right of set-off. In that case the *overlap* will disappear from our financial statements and only the net amount will appear as either an asset or a liability.

To sum up, currency risk management must fit into the company's normal operating, management, commercial, marketing and financial policies and constraints. These mainstream management functions should not underestimate the importance of the currency environment, but currency management must be conducted in an ancillary role to them.

Summarizing the management principles: a checklist

Having set the scene, we can now summarize the problems and principles of balance sheet risk management against a checklist which follows from what we have discovered in our review of the more detailed issues. The list would be useful to anyone tackling the problem 'from cold'.

1. Currency of measurement

This is usually the reporting currency of each company, and in the case of the group the reporting currency of the parent company. But there are exceptions to this norm, discussed above in Chapter 20.

2. Attitude to risk

Is our corporate posture wholly defensive? Or wholly aggressive? Or at some point between the two? Do we have normal guidelines which avoid or hedge all risk, with an exception procedure which accepts risk or goes aggressively for currency gains provided that this is controlled at a specified level close to the main board? Or do we accept risk in specified currencies or subsidiaries, but not elsewhere? This is further discussed in Chapter 26.

3. Are we concerned with accounting or with true risk?

In Chapter 21 we concluded that this largely concerns the value which we ascribe to fixed assets in quantifying our risk, and how far we decide to manage risk in each subsidiary as compared with world-wide for the whole group. The first of these problems might go away if accounting at current values became universal.

4. How far do we wish to manage risk in each subsidiary?

This problem really falls into two categories. One is how far a parent company wants to see its foreign subsidiary financing its local currency assets with local currency debt, so as to minimize the *group* exposure on that local currency. The other is how far that local company should have exposures in currencies other than its local currency. These could be the parent company's reporting currency or third currencies. The former category concerns the group exposure to the political and economic risks discussed in Chapter 24. The choice is whether to borrow the local currency within the subsidiary (in which case we probably want the subsidiary's net worth to be small) or offshore outside the subsidiary. The latter category concerns possible risk to the subsidiary's solvency or its tax position, which we discussed in Chapters 21 and 24. But it can also affect the display of the effect of currency movements in local and consolidated accounts, and this is also the subject of Chapter 21.

In practice very few groups can afford to manage currency risk only in terms of their world-wide group position, however efficient that concept may be in terms of management effort and dealing expense. We may often be in a position where we have to reduce sterling borrowings in our Italian subsidiary, and yet increase them in our US parent company if we want to be immune to risk from sterling fluctuations. Some authorities would regard such a policy as absurd, but it can be essential to the health of the group.

5. Do we have any political risks to watch?

We looked at this in Chapter 24 in the widest sense. Every country with a less than freely traded, fully convertible currency presents us with some country risk and may prompt us to finance the local subsidiary with little equity and much local debt.

6. Are we up against financial, legal, exchange control, or tax constraints?

In Chapter 24, we looked at some of the more obvious instances, but the constraints could come from loan covenants or the thinness and short maturities of the forward market (Chapter 9) or of the market in borrowings. Many countries impose limits on local borrowings by foreign-controlled companies. This can restrict leading and lagging as well as a policy of keeping the local equity low. In Chapter 24 we looked at the possibility of borrowing a currency which we believe will move closely with the currency which we have difficulty in borrowing; this is called the parallel hedge.

7. Balance sheet risk management devices

The main ones are:

1. borrowing the currencies in which we have excess assets,
2. forward cover,
3. creating deposits in currencies where we have excess liabilities,
4. leading and lagging,
5. intragroup dividend policy, capital increases and reductions, advancing or calling in loans,
6. bilateral forward contracts, swaps, back-to-back or parallel loans with outside parties.

These devices have all been discussed in Chapters 9 to 11 and elsewhere, but they all have their constraints. *Borrowings* are appropriate only when the exposure is positive (that is, more assets than liabilities in the currency), when there are no limits to our borrowing powers, legal, contractual or financial, which would be breached, and when the right funds are available to the right group company on the right terms, which may however include variable rather than fixed interest. Subject to these constraints, however, they are the best of the balance sheet risk management implements. *Forward cover* may well not be available at all, or not for the desired maturity, but it has the advantage that it does not create balance sheet liabilities which could be in breach of covenants. Forward contracts can be rolled over like loans (we looked at this in Example 16 in Chapter 15), provided we can be sure that the forward market will still be there when we need to roll over and provided we are prepared for the cash flow effect at the time of rolling over: borrowings can be rolled over without such a cash settlement. And we have to watch the tax effect in this context (Chapter 24). *Depositing in currencies* where we have a short position is obviously only applicable to a short position, and can of course result in overlapping assets and liabilities (which artificially raises the gearing ratio) and in low interest yields. *Leading and lagging, adjusting intragroup dividend policy, internal capital increases and reductions, increasing or reducing internal loans:* all these are subject to the obvious constraints. Loans can only be repaid to the extent of the amount outstanding, leading and lagging can only be done to the extent of the possible ranges of trade credit (for example, it cannot normally be less than nil), all of them could be restricted by exchange controls or penalized by withholding taxes, and all of them are subject to the availability of refinancing funds to the group company on which that burden is to fall.

Bilateral forward contracts, swaps and loans are rare because it is hard to find two independent commercial parties with equal and opposite requirements, they can cause intricate tax and credit problems, and they are also subject to possible legal restrictions: for example in Brazil foreign-controlled companies cannot lend to each other without the intermediation of a bank. But where these problems can be solved, they can circumvent quite a few shortcomings of the ordinary markets, especially, for example, where the ordinary banking market stretches only to relatively short maximum maturities.

We have quite deliberately not listed those devices which are designed to shift profits or profit margins from one country to another within a group, for reasons set out earlier in this chapter.

The selection of the device which best meets a particular problem is then a matter of looking at the list of devices, and eliminating those which are either not appropriate or run into constraints in our particular case. Many decisions involve difficult judgements about lesser evils.

8. Quantifying the hedge needed for each risk

The biggest problem, concerning our view of the value of the fixed assets, has been covered under item 3 above. But we still have to make sure that we have correctly dealt with the borderline problems outlined in Chapter 19: items covered forward must be treated as being part of the position in the currency *for* which (not *from* which) they have been bought or sold forward; and items which are postnatal commitments but not yet on the balance sheet, must be included. And that includes particularly some capital expenditure purchase orders. We must also bear in mind the tax effect. If currency gains and losses will have different tax effects on the risk and on the hedge, this must be taken into account in assessing the amount of the hedge needed. We looked at a formula for this in Chapter 24.

9. Splitting each risk by maturities

For each non-reporting currency there is only one risk, but this has to be split by maturities. This warrants the use of a netting matrix for each exposed currency. The matrix should not be restricted to trading items like receivables and payables, but should cover the whole exposure in a currency. It may well stretch over several decades, but perhaps grouped into convenient maturity blocks for the longer-dated non-monetary assets or net investment 'islands'.

10. The big timing problem: when to hedge?

Then comes the biggest problem debated in Chapter 23. Do we go into the market *now*? Even if we have reason to think that the big adverse trend in the spot rate has very nearly run its course and may well reverse itself in the near future, so that our action would look ill-timed with the future benefit of hindsight? And in any case, is this a two-horse race (hedge now or not?) or a multihorse race (when between now and maturity can we get the best forward—or spot—rate)? That is perhaps the worst problem in currency risk management along with the risk in the tender period of large contracts.

However, this question should probably not be asked where the risk is not postnatal. In other words, where a significant fresh exposure, in the form of a major expansion project or acquisition is just being taken on as a commitment. This was doubtless done with the benefit of a currency risk analysis. Exchange rates were no doubt used in arriving at a decision, and those rates should be safeguarded by instant market action at the time of the decision. This is not the proper occasion for a multihorse race, or indeed for placing the whole economic justification of the project in jeopardy. Our horse race has to be run only where there is an *existing*, and therefore *unavoidable* risk.

The above checklist might well assist the process of well-informed and appropriate decision-taking in the field of balance sheet currency risk management.

PART 7

Corporate Objectives, Policies and Organization

CHAPTER 26

Corporate Attitudes and Objectives

We have now surveyed the whole field of trading and balance sheet currency risk management. Up to this point we have assumed that each company is concerned at least to know how to manage risk defensively, and to make that its normal rule. The company is then free to take controlled open positions of its own choosing.

We have also stressed that the area which in many companies needs more attention than it is now receiving, is the inception of each risk. This is particularly the case in the field of trading risk where the idea that any financial expert should be involved in pricing decisions, goes against the grain. In the balance sheet area, where most decisions are financing decisions, there is generally a much greater awareness of currency implications, but even here there is often room for either more or prompter attention to currency risk in significant investment and financing decisions.

There are of course many companies whose practice is very close to what is here being recommended. But there is no doubt that a great many other companies have a very different view of currency risk and how they ought to manage it. And they include companies with an excellent record and reputation for the quality of their financial direction. There are, of course, other companies whose practices are the result of much less thought and care, who may simply be following what they believe the majority of others are doing, without any thought of why that majority practice should be valid, or even whether it fits their own particular pattern of operations.

If we tried to identify the reasons why intelligently directed companies reject the views advocated in this book, we might perhaps find that the following thoughts are a fair and perhaps not untypical summary of what is on their minds:

1. Pricing decisions, capital expenditure decisions and so on have to be taken by line managers (or commercial managers) who must be totally responsible for their decisions, accountable for their consequences, and able to make their judgements at commercial speeds so as to respond to the rapidly changing conditions in their markets. We can-

171

not burden them with interference from a host of experts in other subjects, however important they may be.

2. In any event, we do have a strong treasury team who manage our currency exposures, with a good record of success. What is the point of having that team if we do not give it any risks to manage?

3. Moreover, our particular trading risks are unavoidable in any case. Our major cost is the purchase of cocoa (or copper or tobacco leaf); we have no choice about the currency in which we pay for that, and that is not the currency in which we can sell to all our customers. Even if we could, our other costs like wages, rent, energy, have to be paid for here in our domestic currency, and that is not the currency in which we buy the commodity. So we are stuck with our currency risk, and no currency expert can get us out of that problem.

4. If we need a new machine, we need the best machine with the greatest capacity and the most modern labour-saving features. It happens to come from Germany. We do not need currency advice to tell us that the D-mark is strong and that it might save us a few per cent of buying cost if we bought a British or Italian machine instead. We know that. But that extra cost is minimal compared with the overall effect on production costs if we do not buy the German machine.

5. Besides, we do not really believe in a defensive attitude to currencies. We want to make money out of them. And we do.

This last point goes of course to the root of one of the management conundrums. A manufacturer of soap cannot help producing glycerine as a byproduct. At a senior management conference of an international leader in this field a speaker had argued that for the convenience of the soap department the glycerine department was being deprived of some substantial profit opportunities. He was corrected by a managing director who said 'Gentlemen, we are here to make soap, not glycerine'. The managing director was in his turn corrected by an even more senior executive of the parent company: 'No, gentlemen, we are not here to make soap, but to make money'. This dialogue is echoed in many places where a treasurer is told quite firmly that his company is here to make and market food products, not currency gains. And in some companies there is a parent company finance director who disagrees, on the grounds that profits, from whatever source, must come first.

That is a major issue on which we must remain neutral.

But the case which we have just argued for keeping the treasurer out of the antenatal clinic, does seem to rest on some technical misconceptions about the nature of currency gains and losses.

Perhaps it would be useful to classify currency risks for this discussion into:

1. risks created by deliberate, but not necessarily well-informed, deci-

sions made in the course of operating the business (like a decision to sell in a currency other than that of cost);
2. involuntary operating risks not expertly managed at inception: buying coffee in dollars and setting selling prices in lire without buying the dollars forward or looking beyond the present spot rate for dollars at which the currency deal is unlikely to be done;
3. risks that we are stuck with for the time being, like a large excess of assets over liabilities in South African rand, Australian dollars, or Indian rupees;
4. risks that we could deliberately open up, like borrowing a substantial sum of sterling to convert into a yen deposit, if we believe the yen to be due for a major appreciation (assuming for this purpose that the group has no significant assets or sales or purchases in yen).

Currency management resources are scarce and expensive. If our company believes that its team of experts should earn its keep by making some money for the company, the team could do this most effectively by trying to make profits out of the (4) category, devoting some thought to the solution of the risks in (3), and advising the decision takers in (1) and (2) on how to take good defensive decisions, supplying them with market information about forward rates and other important technical matters.

At the same time the team could be freed from the thankless and time-consuming task of managing a heavy load of undesirable or hitherto neglected exposures under (1) and (2). In the cases of (1) and (2) there is no doubt that currency expertise applied in the process of conception and birth can do far more good at the cost of far less work.

One vital point which must be repeated here is that it is quite possible for the opposition to score a goal even if we take our eyes off the ball for only a short time. If we take a pricing decision this morning, and the treasurer gets to hear about it this afternoon, it is quite possible that the currency will have moved away beyond retrieval in those few dealing hours from where we can achieve the currency result (or better), that we built into the pricing decision. This is an extreme way of putting it, but in the case of a large tender, in the case of all antenatal risk, and indeed in all cases where a risk has been accepted, we cannot afford to take a chance on when the currency management team will become aware of it. They ought to be aware of it before it is a commitment.

Nor is this just a timing point. It is not just that we cannot afford to take our eye off the ball for a short period. It is also that we cannot afford to take uninformed decisions. The very minimum which is desirable here is that the decision-takers should be aware of the forward rates at which the pricing decision could be made to achieve its intended result. If the forward rate is worse than the spot rate (for example, if the currency in which we want to sell stands at a forward discount to the currency of cost), then we must allow for that extra cost. If the forward rate is more favourable to us than the spot rate, then we need to be aware that not only we, but our competitors too, can get some extra margin out of it which we can take either as extra profit or as price reduction to ensure we get the contract or some additional market share. This is a vital piece of *commercial* intelligence without which we may not survive in cut-throat markets. And yet it comes from currency expertise.

Now, what about the point that commercial decisions must be taken by people who take full responsibility for their decisions and the acumen of their judgement, who can take them at commercial speeds without unnecessary consultations with experts? And of course in the need for full accountability: there is no hiding behind the veto of the treasurer. What about that?

This too is a misunderstanding. Let us say that we are a manufacturer of a consumer product in the United States and we import an item from England which costs around one-third of our dollar selling price. Our overall net profit margin is fairly low and very vulnerable to any cost changes in the imported content. The market is competitive. The spot rate at a point where we wish to obtain a large order from a good customer is $2 = £1. Our case is that the manager who decides on the dollar price of the offer should first have a word with the currency expert. But it is no part of the treasurer's job to tell the manager what decision to take. His job is to find out how soon after taking the business the British goods will have to be paid for, and to look up the forward rate for that time-lag. It could be that this will reduce the dollar cost of the component by 5%; for the forward rate is only $1.90. Next he has to point out that if the company cannot yet take a chance on needing those British goods, before it has landed the order, the dollar/sterling rate can move up. If it is a week before the British goods can be ordered, then it could go up to (say) $2.10 and a worst-case forward rate might be $2.02. He might also do well to check with the commercial manager that there is no alternative supplier in the United States who might charge less than $2.02 for an equally good component; secondly, that the British supplier could not be induced to quote in dollars, and thirdly, that the big US customer might not be willing to accept a lower price based on a buying cost at $1.90, with a sterling variation clause giving him the full benefit of the forward rate in return for leaving us with no risk.

The odds are that our commercial manager will reluctantly tell us that none of these options are commercially possible, so that he will go in and fix his price on the assumption of a buying cost at $2.02. And the pair of them should then agree to keep in touch in case anything dramatically changes on either front, such as a major delay in the quotation (in which case the treasurer should be asked to update his rate at the appropriate time) or a major change in the dollar/sterling rate (in which case the commercial manager should be informed about the new threat or opportunity which this may bring about.)

None of this dialogue constitutes an interference in the decision by the currency expert. It merely conveys information of vital commercial significance to the manager who decides the price. It does not confuse the subsequent accountability for the commercial decision. The commercial manager accepts $2.02 as his given currency cost, and answers for the consequences of his judgement *on that assumption*. The treasurer accepts responsibility for that rate of $2.02, and answers for any professional defect or incompetence that may have been involved in that judgement on his part. Far from fudging responsibilities, this identifies and clarifies them. And the procedure is designed to ensure that the risk is hedged as soon as it is born. The commercial trading account will show the results of the commercial decisions, not a mixture of the results of those decisions and of the currency gains and losses which might occur until the treasurer does finally get to hear about the risks and either manages them or takes them over into his own finance company or currency trading account. For that interval is the one in which shirts have been lost.

Obviously this procedure would be uneconomic and unrealistic if we applied it to every currency pricing decision in a company which has a very large number of such decisions, most of them relatively small. If this was an unavoidable feature of its business, the consultation procedures would have to be restricted to the larger pricing decisions. Experience shows that where sales are relatively numerous but of small individual size, there are nevertheless surprisingly few pricing decisions. Such decisions take the form of issuing price lists or minimum price lists. In such businesses very few real pricing decisions are made in any period; so few in fact that it would be foolish to deprive them of the benefit of currency expertise if they involve an exchange rate judgement. And of course, even in a company with a very large number of unavoidable pricing decisions, they do not necessarily all of them have to involve a currency mismatch, and one of the objects of consultation is precisely to see whether the number of currency risks could with advantage be reduced. Obviously, where we are still left with highly fragmented and dispersed decision-taking in this field, the best contribution for the treasurer to make is to train as many people as possible at each decision point to understand how the currency market works, to ascertain up-to-date information about forward and other rates, and to act as decentralized currency experts subject to consultation with the treasurer on difficult problems and with the aid perhaps of brief bulletins circulated by him on current developments in the markets and forecasts of possible future trends. But all this involves both costs and hazards, and in most companies it will be found that the number of unavoidable and significant currency pricing decisions is not very great.

Finally, it may be worth reflecting on why companies are so intent on making money from operating risks (which they might have avoided or hedged at their inception) rather than from risks of their own choice, like the yen exposure in category (4) that we looked at earlier in this chapter. It is of course quite possible that aggressively minded companies found that they were restricted to operating exposures at some past time as a result of exchange controls. For example, companies in the United Kingdom until 1979 could not even have operated foreign currency accounts unless they were kept in credit and within their currency purchase requirements over the following month. In such an environment, companies can hardly set about making money out of currencies if they do not fully use their operating exposures and indeed maximize the number of those exposures so as to create opportunities for profit. More fortunate companies may never have experienced such constraints. They may perhaps shy away from deliberate exposures in a currency in which their business operations are not conducted, but it is hard to see the logic whereby they consider it legitimate to leave their operational risks unhedged in that case. There is a strong case for the company which thinks its job is to make and market food products, not to make money out of currencies. The case is that its equity stockholders may well be supporting the company because they value its ability to make money out of food products rather than currencies. But that logic points towards a defensive currency risk policy in all fields, not just in some.

We can sum up this discussion about financial currency risk by suggesting that there is a strong case for fundamentally defensive policies in ordinary business operations. Currency risk expertise will then be needed to counsel on the avoidance of unnecessary risk, on the management of antenatal and other necessary risk, and to manage any deliberate currency risk which was taken not for operational, but for currency management reasons: to make money for the shareholders. Not every company will wish to do this. But those that do, should make money the easy way, and not the hard way. And the hard way is to try to make money out of whatever exposures drop out of the commercial and other operations.

Economic risks

We defined economic risk in Chapter 3 as the effect of *real* movements in the currency in which we incur our costs, on the competitive position of those costs. It is caused by the real, inflation-adjusted exchange rate, not with the nominal rate with which we are concerned in financial risk. Some authorities consider that the economic risk needs to be managed just as much as financial risks have to be managed. We have not taken that view in this book simply because the economic risk cannot be managed *in its own right*. Every business needs either a formal or an informal marketing and planning function, and this function must assess the whole of the economic climate affecting the demand and supply of its product range. Currency risk is an important element, but no more than an element in that task. It affects prices, costs, and therefore margins and market share. It must be taken into account in every investment decision, in product and market strategy. It would go beyond our scope in this study to follow that recognition up in greater detail.

CHAPTER 27

How to Set Corporate Objectives, Policies and Procedures

In Chapter 26 we looked at the philosophy of the choice between aggress-ive and defensive risk management in the currency field. In this chapter we look at how a company may arrive at rational objectives, and policies and procedures to implement them.

All organizations bear marks of the personalities who effectively run them, but in the matter of currency risk an important part is also played by some more objective factors, which include the nature of the company's business, its competition and its markets, the legal and fiscal environ-ment in which it operates, the skills and other resources at its command, and its existing organization structure.

In this book we have found that currency risk is an important and not always adequately recognized part of the business environment, but that it is only a part of that environment, and not a predominant part. We have said that it cannot become the tail that wags the dog. A way must be found to integrate the management of this risk into the normal management structure and activity, so as to enable a group of companies to achieve its commercial and financial objectives better and with greater safety. And this integration has to be achieved as unobtrusively and cheaply as possible.

Up to Chapter 24 we discussed the topic mainly as it might affect the treasurer in his professional management responsibility. In these last two chapters we are looking at it more from the point of view of how it affects the top management of the group. Top management may of course have a very detailed grasp of the problems. But for those cases where specialist knowledge of the topic is not available at that level, we have to cover the following points:

1. The information which should be available to top management so that objectives can be formulated.
2. Fundamental policy choices.
3. Subsidiary policy choices.
4. Choices about currency management resources.
5. Authority levels for acceptance of risks.
6. Feedback and monitoring.

What top management needs to know in order to formulate objectives

The short, but unhelpful answer to this question is that top management have to know enough to enable them to make well-informed choices about the other five topics.

The first need is for a simple exposition, in non-technical language, of the technical nature of trading and balance sheet risk. This must be done in such a way as to enable top management to form a balanced view of the size of possible losses, of the catastrophe thresholds of risk from the point of view of the group, of the extent to which forecasting skills or services can help to control, mitigate or exploit the risks, of the organizational implications especially where risk management may necessitate interfaces between currency expertise and marketing and pricing activities, and of the implications of currency risk for strategic planning and financial policy.

The second task may well be a memorandum setting out the main choices, and alternative sets of responses to the choices. For example, the more aggressive the policy, the greater will be the resources needed to implement such a policy successfully. So the more aggressive alternatives would be coupled with greater recommended resource allocations.

If outside advisers are used for the task, it is important that they should not belong to organizations who have specific solutions to sell. Many banks are in that category. Banks have a particular perspective of currency risk which gives them unique insights into currency problems, but the perspective and the insights are not usually those of the manufacturing or trading business. For example, the time-span of a bank's view of currency risk is by no means identical with the time-span, or the range of time-spans, which manufacturers have to consider. There cannot be many treasurers who have not been the target of a sales drive by a bank for a brilliant solution to a problem which the treasurer and his company do not happen to have.

Again, no outside consultant can give helpful advice, unless he has had an opportunity to study from the inside how the company operates commercially and financially. The ideal person to advise the board is a company executive who knows the company thoroughly and who has professional knowledge of currency markets and problems. But he must be able to take an objective and detached view.

It is worth stressing here that in many companies the least understood aspect of currency risk is trading risk. Obviously the companies with large export contracts are bound to be aware of it. But in all companies it is an impediment to the understanding of trading risk that trading gains and losses are not usually statistically known. The underlying difficulty is that the exchange rates which went into original pricing decisions are not needed as an input for producing financial accounts or even variance statements against annual budgets. Their significance is just analytical, and they serve only this one purpose: to monitor how sensible the exchange rate assumptions were, and how successfully the company has fought against doing worse than those rates. But if we cannot measure our success or failure, then we are not likely to attend to the topic adequately.

The fundamental choices

We have to look separately at trading and balance sheet risk here. Balance sheet risk is closely related to financing, investment and corporate planning decisions, and these are usually more centralized than trading and pricing decisions. The central control of balance sheet risk would therefore be easier, if desired, than that of trading risk.

The corporate attitude to trading risk

1. Do we turn down all business which involves selling in currencies other than those of cost?
2. Or do we accept antenatal risk only, and other risks too, provided that all risks are fully hedged by the time they become a commercial commitment (that is, at birth)?
3. Or do we accept antenatal risks only in selected currencies?
4. Or do we accept unhedged risks in selected currencies because we judge them to be strong, so that the risks are likely to result in gains?
5. Or do we go one step further and look on currency risk as a profit opportunity, taking *ad hoc* decisions whether and how much to hedge with an eye more on profit than on the avoidance of losses?
6. Or do we believe we can afford to be unselective because our main currency of cost is too weak to warrant the effort of selection?
7. How do we resolve or avoid conflicts between commercial and currency risk objectives?

The corporate attitude to balance sheet risk

Where does the company stand on the scale ranging between wholly aggressive and wholly defensive management of balance sheet risk?

1. Is it the company's policy to match assets and liabilities in all currencies other than the parent reporting currency? Will this principle be taken to the extreme length of avoiding investment in

countries whose currencies are not available as borrowings to finance the investment, and divesting where the objective cannot be achieved, or no longer be achieved?

2. If we do not go to that extreme, is our general approach nevertheless defensive and averse to risk? What criteria do we apply to the acceptance of exposure, for example:

   (a) an intensive marketing need to invest in the territory?
   (b) a minimum rate of return to compensate for possible currency losses?
   (c) a selective currency assessment, such that we have reason to regard the currency as stronger than the parent reporting currency?
   (d) risk-spreading portfolio considerations?

3. Do we regard balance sheet risk as an opportunity to exploit rather than as a risk to avoid? If so, is our policy

   (a) one of controlled risks in selected currencies?
   (b) one of controlled risks in any currency?
   (c) one of taking currency positions unselectively on the grounds that our parent reporting currency is so weak that currency selectivity is unnecessary?

4. Do we measure our success or failure in handling or avoiding balance sheet risk in terms of what shows up in our annual accounts, or in true terms (this question may not arise if there is no conflict)?

5. For what time horizon do we want to manage balance sheet risk? The next reporting date, or the full duration (as the board sees it) of each risk?

6. Has the board any priorities as between short-term and long-term responsibilities and objectives in this field?

7. How strongly does the company wish to avoid political risks generally, and blocked profits and trade receivables in particular?

Subsidiary policy choices

These tend to be concerned with resources and organizational conflicts.

1. In the trading risk field the biggest choice is whether the company is willing to involve currency expertise in difficult pricing decisions. We have seen in Chapter 13 that a hedged foreign currency price may give us a better result in our home currency than the customer would pay us in that home currency. It could be the other way round with a customer who prefers to cover forward himself. But it takes high-powered marketing *and* currency skills to spot and manage

182

these decisions. Where a company has many pricing decisions involving currency problems, it may be uneconomic to bring currency
skill into all of them. But many companies have relatively few of
these decisions. Often they are grouped when price lists are determined. Contracting companies with few very large contracts have no
choice but to involve currency skill every time. This principle should
be (but is not always) extended to all cases where antenatal risk is
involved. But where a company has a great multitude of widely
dispersed pricing decisions, none of them antenatal, it may have to
restrict the availability of currency skills to the largest and potentially catastrophic risks—or embark on a policy of avoidance.

2. Where a company selects one of the more mechanistic policies, like
accepting risks only for D-mark receipts or lira purchases, it must
lay down how often the judgements about those currencies need to
be reviewed and at what level of authority.

3. How far can currency considerations be allowed to override decentralized management authority, and the motivation which goes with
that principle? For example, is the company willing to lead and lag,
and face the problems which this may cause with intercompany
payment disciplines, for example, when a foreign subsidiary is in-
structed to pay faster?

4. How far is the parent company concerned to protect individual companies in the group, as distinct from the group as a whole, from
currency losses?

5. Is the corporate centre concerned about the currency risk in purchasing decisions? If purchasing is a decentralized function, to what
extent is the corporate centre willing to intervene or assist? Should
there be a preference for subcontracts to be placed with subcontractors willing to supply in the currency in which the main contract
price is determined? Will any interface between central currency
expertise and decentralized purchasing judgement weaken the sense
of responsibility of buying departments?

6. Do capital project analysis procedures have to be modified to guard
against falsification of the cost assumptions built into the project
analysis if significant purchases are to be made in foreign currency?

7. As regards balance sheet risk, is the company concerned mainly
with the effect on net worth (after tax), or with particular lines in
the profit and loss account or with changes in reserves (assuming
that the company is to some extent concerned with the *accounting*
effects of currency risk)?

8. To what extent is the company concerned to let currency considerations influence its financial policy on borrowings, dividends from
subsidiaries, required return on capital, taxation, etc.?

9. In what currency does the company measure its performance against

its main competitors? Is this different from the parent reporting currency?

10. What is the company's priority between optimizing interest expense and income on the one hand and currency risk management on the other? Does the company look at the conflicting considerations after tax? And does this involve a trade-off between short-term and longer-term objectives?

11. What is the company's preference for fixed rates of interest, and does it rank before currency risk management objectives?

12. Are there any circumstances in which the company is willing to accept blocked funds in another country, and if so what are those circumstances?

13. If there is to be any aggressive management of receivables, payables and other unhedged trading risks, will the results be accounted for in the trading profit centres? If not, who will be accountable, and by what accounting arrangements? For example, will all receivables and payables be transferred to a central finance company?

14. How does the board see the criteria of success or failure in balance sheet risk management?

Resourcing choices

The resources needed for currency risk management are mainly inhouse staff, external consultancy or services, and internal reporting and data processing about risks. The expert staff may be required for two tasks, risk management (making judgements and decisions) and dealing (getting the best rates to implement decisions).

The choices depend not only on how aggressive or defensive the policies are, but also on the nature of the company's business. A large civil construction company engaged on very large overseas projects handles enormous risks, but relatively few. Its reporting system is almost certainly a contract accounting system. The currency problems are crucial, but a few highly expert executives can often handle them with very little support staff and with no significant extra data requirements. A pharmaceutical business is probably at the opposite end of the scale with a myriad of small risk problems involving a lot of data and a large capability for handling judgements and decisions if risks are to be managed aggressively.

One of the main problems here may be the extent to which the corporate treasurer is to handle exposures in subsidiaries outside his own country. All the choices here are expensive. To hire expertise in a presumably smaller overseas operation may be costly in relation to the size of the task: to give the corporate centre online access to the decisions and the surrounding facts can also be very costly in telephone, telex and travel time.

Authority levels for acceptance of risks

Everything said so far about the nature of currency risks and the management problems suggests that wholly aggressive postures are unlikely to suit many businesses, and that the optimum responses to the fundamental choices are likely to be somewhere near the defensive end of the spectrum, even if not perhaps at the 100% defensive end.

If we look at those solutions with an eye on the resources needed to deal with them, an obviously attractive organization concept is that of management by exception. The concept works through a rule-book or instruction which lays down that risk of various specified kinds may not be accepted without reference to a specified higher authority via the treasurer, or to the treasurer, who in his turn has the task of ensuring that all the salient facts are available, market and other currency facts brought to bear upon them, and then either dealt with by him or referred to higher authority under clearly stated authority levels. The system permits the clearance of risks by category (for example, all sales by the Italian subsidiary in D-marks, and perhaps all risks which are hedged at birth without an antenatal period).

Such a procedure has the enormous virtue of restricting the risk management effort to relatively few risks (because the norm is avoidance by matching or hedging at birth) and probably the more difficult and worthwhile problems, and of ensuring that there is a dialogue with the treasurer, for example about difficult pricing decisions. A good treasurer will soon be seen as an ally rather than an obstruction to profitable sales effort. Particularly in those many situations where the proposed currency of sale is at a premium to the currency of cost, the treasurer can often point out attractive pricing opportunities which only the currency expert is likely to spot. These are the incidental bonuses of having a system of management by exception under which currency risks are not accepted without a prior processing through staff skilled in the matter.

Such a rule-book will, of course, also specify what risks need to go back to the main board, or are delegated to the finance director or the treasurer or perhaps a committee of appropriate executives. It should, however, be stressed that committee procedures are more appropriate to balance sheet than to trading risks. Trading risks are usually too urgent for such a procedure.

Feedback and monitoring

This is not a satisfactory topic, because no satisfactory principles exist for it. And the reason for that is that no-one has yet found satisfactory or universally applicable criteria for measuring the success or failure of currency risk management. In other words, what is par for the course? It is easy to give ourselves a small hurdle to jump, but much more difficult to formulate a universally appropriate performance standard.

Where the policy of the company is to manage trading risks as trading risks, that is, to aim at doing no worse than the rate at which the pricing decision was taken, the criterion is readymade, and the only problem is the minor one of recording all the exchange rates used in pricing decisions, and comparing them with the outturn. There is no question of having to judge performance against the best available rate during the life of the exposure.

That question, however, does arise with balance sheet exposure, where every decision, after the first significant financing decision at least, involves a timing element.

It is not reasonable to expect mere human currency risk managers to attain this criterion, and it is necessary to give them reasonably achievable tasks and a manageable workload. This is one more reason for taking a fairly defensive posture.

However, the monitoring problem remains. Subject to the specific criteria chosen by the company, the best procedure seems to be to define the risk management tasks, to decide the available resources, and then to lay down just what standard of performance can be expected of those resources. The monitoring should then consist of periodical records of

1. what risks are outstanding at each review date;
2. how those risks compare with those outstanding on previous dates;
3. decisions taken at this review date, with brief reasons;
4. review of past decisions and the reasons for those.

The records will have limited value for the assessment of performance, but properly conducted reviews will no doubt show the weaknesses and strengths of past decisions and improve the quality of future decision-taking. The main board should obviously at least receive quarterly or annual reports of all outstanding risks.

Conclusion

It is evident that top management has many difficult questions to resolve and directives to give. The most difficult may be the interrelation between the currency risk management function and other financial and commercial operations. Particularly in the commercial pricing field, it may be tempting to draw a parallel with credit control, where conflict between commercial aims and financially perceived risk may also occur. But there are important differences. Currency risk is more concealed, more technical in nature, and the management techniques depend on specialized markets.

Reluctantly we must conclude that currency risk is different from other risks and needs its own management resources and methods. The greatest need is for it to be correctly recognized for what it is, for objectives and policies to be set, and for its management to be properly integrated into the management structure of the organization.

Index